A Traverse Theatre Company, Theatre Royal Bath Ustinov Studio
and Bush Theatre co-production

# Right Now

**by Catherine-Anne Toupin, translated by Chris Campbell**

Directed by Michael Boyd

*Right Now* by Catherine-Anne Toupin,
translated by Chris Campbell

## COMPANY LIST

### CAST

**ALICE** – Lindsey Campbell
**BEN** – Sean Biggerstaff
**JULIETTE** – Maureen Beattie
**FRANÇOIS** – Dyfan Dwyfor
**GILLES** – Guy Williams

### CREATIVE TEAM

Playwright – **CATHERINE-ANNE TOUPIN**
Translator – **CHRIS CAMPBELL**
Director – **MICHAEL BOYD**
Designer – **MADELEINE GIRLING**
Lighting Designer – **OLIVER FENWICK**
Composer/Sound Designer – **DAVID PAUL JONES**
Casting Director – **GINNY SCHILLER CDG**
Casting Assistant – **LIZ BICHARD / AMY BEADEL**
Assistant Director – **CHLOE MASTERTON**

### PRODUCTION TEAM

Production Manager – **KEVIN MCCALLUM**
Company Stage Manager – **DAVID SNEDDON**
Deputy Stage Manager – **VICKY WILSON**
Costume Supervisor – **KAT SMITH**

## COMPANY BIOGRAPHIES

### Maureen Beattie (JULIETTE)

Maureen trained at RSAMD and graduated with the James Bridie Gold Medal. Since then she has gone on to play many roles with companies across the UK including the National Theatre of Scotland, National Theatre of Great Britain, the Globe, and the RSC, as well as touring internationally.

Previous theatre credits include: *The List, The Carousel, The Deliverance* (Stellar Quines); *Yer Granny, 27 and The Enquirer* (National Theatre of Scotland); *Romeo & Juliet* (Rose Theatre Kingston); *Dark Road, The Cherry Orchard* (Royal Lyceum Edinburgh); *Noises Off* (The Old Vic Tour); *No Quarter* (Royal Court Theatre); *The Skin of Our Teeth* (Young Vic); *Ghosts, Acting Up* (Citizens Theatre); *Medea, Oedipus, Electra* (Theatre Babel); The *Masterbuilder* (Chichester); *Othello, The Merry Wives of Windsor* (National Theatre) and *The Histories Cycle, Richard III, Titus Andronicus, Macbeth, King Lear, The Constant Couple* (Royal Shakespeare Company).

Maureen's television and film credits include: *Outlander, Doctor Who, Vera, Casualty, Lewis, Midsomer Murders, Taggart, Bramwell, The Bill, Hard to Get, The Worst Week of My Life, Doctors, Moving On, Ruffian Hearts* and *The Decoy Bride.*

### Sean Biggerstaff (BEN)

Sean obtained his first professional acting role at ten, playing the son of MacDuff in a Michael Boyd production of *Macbeth* at the Tron Theatre, Glasgow. Other theatre work includes: *Solid Air* (Theatre Royal Plymouth); *The Girl with the Red Hair* (Lyceum/Bush/Hampstead Theatre); *An Appointment with the Wicker Man* (National Theatre of Scotland).

Sean's film work includes: *Whisky Galore, CASHBACK, Harry Potter and the Philosopher's Stone, Harry Potter and the Chamber of Secrets* and *Harry Potter and the Deathly Hallows (Part 2)* playing the part of Oliver Wood. His television work includes: *Marple, Charles II,* and *Consenting Adults* for which he won BAFTA Scotland's Best Actor Award for his performance.

### Michael Boyd (DIRECTOR)

Michael Boyd was Artistic Director of the Royal Shakespeare Company from 2002 to 2012, where his productions included the twenty four hour *RSC Histories Cycle*, winner of four Olivier Awards. He led the £112 million reconstruction of the Royal Shakespeare Theatre, as well as commissioning and producing the Complete Works Festival 2006-7, the World Shakespeare Festival for the London Olympics 2012, and *Matilda the Musical*. He took a repertoire of seven Shakespeare plays to the Park Avenue Armory as part of the Lincoln Center Festival, New York, in 2011. Prior to joining the RSC, he was founding Artistic Director of the Tron Theatre in Glasgow from 1985 to 1996, where his productions included *The Guid Sisters* and *The Real World?* by the Québécois playwright Michel Tremblay, Ted Hughes' *Crow, The Trick Is To Keep Breathing* (also Royal Court and World Stage Festival, Toronto), and *Macbeth*. In 2014/15 he staged both parts of Marlowe's *Tamburlaine* in New York (Obie, Drama

Desk, and Drama League Awards), and made his Royal Opera debut with Monteverdi's *Orfeo* at the Roundhouse (nominated, Outstanding Achievement in Opera, Olivier Awards).

He has been Visiting Professor at the University of Michigan, and the Cameron Mackintosh Professor of Contemporary Theatre at the University of Oxford, where he is a Fellow of St Catherine's College. He was knighted for services to drama in 2012.

### Chris Campbell (TRANSLATOR)

Chris is currently Literary Manager of the Royal Court after being Deputy Literary Manager of the National Theatre for six years. He has translated plays by Philippe Minyana, David Lescot, Rémi de Vos, Adeline Picault, Magali Mougel, Launcelot Hamelin, Frédéric Blanchette, Catherine-Anne Toupin and Fabrice Roger-Lacan for the National, the Almeida, the Donmar, the Traverse, the Birmingham Rep and the Young Vic among others. In 2014, Chris was appointed Chevalier de l'Ordre des Arts et des Lettres by the French government. An actor for many years, Chris has worked at many theatres including the National, the Birmingham Rep, the Gate and the Traverse. He most recently appeared alongside Meryl Streep in *The Iron Lady*.

### Lindsey Campbell (ALICE)

Lindsey trained at the Royal Central School of Speech and Drama, graduating in 2013.

Previous stage credits include: *Nights* (White Bear Theatre); *The Harvest* (Ustinov Studio, Theatre Royal Bath/Soho Theatre); *The Big Meal* (Theatre Royal Bath/Hightide) and *A Christmas Carol* (Royal Lyceum Theatre).

Film and television credits include: *Casualty*, *Doctor's*, *Dani's House*, *Blue Haven*, *Single Father*, *The Holly Kane Experiment* and *Intergalactic Kitchen*.

### Dyfan Dwyfor (FRANÇOIS)

Dyfan graduated from the Royal Welsh College of Music & Drama in 2007. He won the Richard Burton Award at the National Eisteddfod in 2004.

Most recently he has appeared in *Candylion* (National Theatre Wales). Other theatre credits include: *The Harvest* (Ustinov Studio, Theatre Royal Bath/Soho Theatre); *Titus Andronicus* (The Globe); *Praxis Makes Perfect* (National Theatre Wales); *Too Clever by Half* (Royal Exchange); *Fortunes Fool* (The Old Vic); *Ahasverus, Hamlet, Little Eagles, Romeo & Juliet*, *The Drunks, As You Like It, Comedy of Errors* (RSC).

Film and Television work includes: *Yr Oedi*, *Hinterland*, *Caerdydd*, *A470*, *Y Llyfrgell*, *The Passing, I Know You Know* and *The Baker* and *Pride*.

### Oliver Fenwick (LIGHTING DESIGNER)

Theatre includes: *Love's Labour's Lost, Much Ado About Nothing, The Jew of Malta, Wendy and Peter Pan, The Winter's Tale, The Taming Of The Shrew, Julius Caesar, The Drunks, The Grain Store* (RSC); *The Motherf\*\*ker With The Hat, The Holy Rosenburgs, The Passion, Happy*

*Now?* (National Theatre); *Lela & Co, Routes, The Witness, Disconnect* (Royal Court); *The Vote, Berenice, Huis Clos* (Donmar Warehouse); *My City, Ruined* (Almeida); *Multitudes, Red Velvet, Paper Dolls, Bracken Moor, Handbagged* (Tricycle Theatre); *Di and Viv And Rose, Handbagged, The Importance of Being Earnest, Bakersfield Mist, The Madness Of George III, Ghosts, Kean, The Solid Gold Cadillac, Secret Rapture* (All West End); *To Kill A Mockingbird* (Tour & Barbican); *The King's Speech* (Tour); *After Miss Julie* (Young Vic); *Saved, A Midsummer Night's Dream* (Lyric, Hammersmith); *To Kill A Mockingbird, Hobson's Choice, The Beggars Opera* (Regents Park Theatre); *Therese Raquin, The Big Meal, King Lear, Candida* (Bath); *The Whipping Man* (Plymouth); *Into The Woods, Sunday In The Park With George* (Chatelet Theatre, Paris); *The Kitchen Sink, The Contingency Plan, If There is I Haven't Found It Yet* (Bush Theatre); *A Number, Travel With My Aunt* (Chocolate Factory); *Private Lives, The Giant; Glass Eels; Comfort Me With Apples* (Hampstead theatre); *Restoration* (Headlong); *Pride And Prejudice, Hamlet, The Caretaker, Comedy of Errors, Bird Calls, Iphigenia* (Crucible Theatre, Sheffield).

Opera includes: *Werther* (Scottish Opera); *The Merry Widow* (Opera North & Sydney Opera House); *Samson et Delilah, Lohengrin, The Trojan Trilogy, The Nose, The Gentle Giant* (Royal Opera House).

## Madeleine Girling (DESIGNER)

Madeleine Girling trained in Theatre Design at The Royal Welsh College of Music and Drama, graduating with a First Class Honors, and receiving The Lord Williams Memorial Prize for Design 2012. In 2013 she was awarded as a winner in *The Linbury Prize For Stage Design* for her collaboration with Nottingham Playhouse. Between April 2013 and July 2014 she worked for The Royal Shakespeare Company in a one-year, Design Assistant position. Previous design work includes: *A Skull in Connemara* (Nottingham Playhouse); *The Harvest* (Ustinov Studio, Theatre Royal Bath/Soho Theatre); *Little Light* (The Orange Tree Theatre); *The Chronicles of Kalki* (Gate Theatre); *Time And The Conways*; *Arcadia* (Nottingham Playhouse); *Revolt. She Said. Revolt Again.*; *The Ant & The Cicada* (Royal Shakespeare Company); *Gardening for the Unfulfilled and Alienated* (Undeb Theatre); *Tender Napalm*; *How To Curse* (BOVTS Director's Showcase); *A Welshman's Guide To Breaking Up* (Boyo Productions); *Hey Diddle Diddle* (Bristol Old Vic); *The Cagebirds* (LAMDA Director's Showcase); *The Life After* (BOV Young Company); *Blood Wedding* (RWCMD Burton Company).

## David Paul Jones (COMPOSER/SOUND DESIGNER)

David is an Edinburgh-based composer, pianist, vocalist and songwriter. His work for Theatre includes: *Tracks of The Winter Bear, The Tree Of Knowledge* and *Bloody Trams* (Traverse); *Those Eyes, That Mouth, The Devil's Larder, Barflies* and *What Remains* (Grid Iron); *Butterfly* (Ramesh Meyyappan); *World Factory* (Metis/Young Vic); *Elizabeth Gordon Quinn, Something Wicked This Way Comes, Mary Queen Of Scots Got Her Head Chopped Off, Our Teacher's A Troll, Dolls, The Missing* (National Theatre of Scotland); *Great Expectations* (Dundee Rep); *Pobby & Dingan* and *Caged* (Catherine Wheels).

David has worked internationally on projects in Australia, South America, USA, Middle East, Singapore and, most recently, as composer for the National Theatre of China in Beijing and Hong Kong.

David is the recipient of several awards including the Glenfiddich Spirit of Scotland Award for Music. His recorded work is available on Linn Records and www.davidpauljones.com

## Chloe Masterton (ASSISTANT DIRECTOR)

Chloe is currently studying for an MA in Drama Directing at the Bristol Old Vic Theatre School.

As director her credits include: *A Doll's House* (Bristol Old Vic Theatre School); *Track* and *Threads* (Bierkeller New Writing Festival); *The Vagina Monologues* (Bierkeller) and *The Wing* (Bristol Old Vic Basement/Theatre Uncut).

As assistant director her credits include: *Wind in the Willows* (Bristol Old Vic Theatre School); *The Eleventh Hour, The Imaginaries* and *Nordost* (The Egg, Theatre Royal Bath).

## Ginny Schiller CDG (CASTING DIRECTOR)

Ginny has been Casting Director for the Royal Shakespeare Company, Chichester Festival Theatre, Rose Theatre Kingston, English Touring Theatre and Soho Theatre. She has worked on many shows for the West End and No. 1 touring circuit as well as for the Almeida, Arcola, Bath Theatre Royal, Birmingham Rep, Bolton Octagon, Bristol Old Vic, Clwyd Theatr Cymru, Frantic Assembly, Greenwich Theatre, Hampstead Theatre, Headlong, Liverpool Everyman and Playhouse, Lyric Theatre Belfast, Menier Chocolate Factory, Northampton Royal & Derngate, Oxford Playhouse, Plymouth Theatre Royal and Drum, Regent's Park Open Air Theatre, Shared Experience, Sheffield Crucible, Young Vic, West Yorkshire Playhouse and Wilton's Music Hall. She has also worked on many television, film and radio productions.

Previous work for the Theatre Royal, Bath includes: *The Father* (also West End/tour); *She Stoops to Conquer, Talking Heads, Hay Fever* and *Relative Values* (both also West End); *Kafka's Dick, Thérèse Raquin, Bad Jews* (also West End/tour); *The Hypochondriac, Things We Do For Love, Moon Tiger, The Tempest, Hysteria, Home, This Happy Breed* and *Born in the Gardens*. She has cast all bar one of the previous Ustinov Studio productions under Laurence Boswell's artistic directorship.

## Catherine-Anne Toupin (PLAYWRIGHT)

Catherine-Anne Toupin is a French Canadian actress and writer. She graduated from The Conservatory of Dramatic Arts in Montreal in 1999. Over the years, Catherine-Anne has become a well-known actress in Quebec. She has acted in more than 30 plays and her resumé includes numerous television and film credits. She can now be seen each week, on CBC, in two popular Quebecois television dramas: *Unité 9* and *Mémoires Vives*. She has also created a half-hour TV comedy entitled *Boomerang,* in which she stars with her fiancé, actor Antoine Bertrand. The show is a huge hit and is already preparing its third season.

As a playwright, Catherine-Anne has written three full-length plays: *À présent*, *L'envie* and *Alexandre,* as well as many short plays. In 2005, *Right Now (À présent)* won the *Prix Françoise-Berd* awarded to the best new play by a young author. The play has been translated into four languages and has been produced in Canada, Italy and Mexico. Catherine-Anne now lives in Montreal where she spends most of her time acting and working as a script editor for her Sitcom *Boomerang*. She hopes to write another play soon …

## Guy Williams (GILLES)

Guy trained at LAMDA and has gone on to perform in a huge range of theatre, television and film roles. Previous theatre credits include: *Spanish Tragedy* (Arcola); *King Lear, The Seagull, The Merry Wives of Windsor, The Winters Tale, The Changeling* (RSC); *The Duchess of Malfi* (West Yorkshire Playhouse); *Present Laughter* (Theatre Clwyd); *Rebecca* (National Tour); *Journey's End* (Comedy); *The Romans in Britain* (Crucible Theatre); *Pravda, The Government Inspector, Venice Preserved, Antigone, Coriolanus,* (National Theatre), *Timon of Athens* (Leicester); *Rose Rage* (Propeller, Watermill, Theatre Royal); *A Midsummer Night's Dream* (Propeller, Watermill, Comedy).

Guy's film credits include: *London Has Fallen, The Man from U.N.C.L.E, The Cosmonaut, Sherlock Holmes, Middleton's Changeling, To Walk With Lions, Thin Ice.* Television work includes: *Indian Summers, Young Cilla, Peaky Blinders, Downton Abbey, Mr Selfridge, Father Brown, Ripper Street, This is England 88, Land Girls, Law and Order, The Queen, Silent Witness, Spooks, King Lear, A Very Social Secretary, Trial and Retribution,* and *Happy Valley.*

---

*Right Now* was first presented in the UK as a script-in-hand reading at the Traverse in November 2014 as part of *New Writing from Quebec*, a cultural exchange between the Traverse Theatre and Théâtre La Licorne, home of La Manufacture Theatre Company, in Montréal. It was then presented in a week of preview performances at the Traverse in May 2015.

The Traverse would like to thank all those involved in the development of *Right Now* on its journey to full UK production this year.

## Special thanks to:

Québec Government Office in London
British Council Canada
Jean-Denis Leduc and all at Théâtre La Licorne
Emma Callander

## Foreword From Translator, Chris Campbell

Most people in the UK who know anything about Québec theatre will be familiar with either Michel Tremblay, the bard of working-class Montreal, or the world-conquering phenomenon that is Robert Lepage.

When I first went there, ten years ago, I was thrilled to discover one of the most vital and particular theatre cultures I've come across. Québec is a francophone island in the middle of an English-speaking ocean and the pride with which they defend their culture is an inspiration. As well as the pressure from the surrounding English Canadians, not to mention the USA to the South, there's a far from straightforward relationship with the French; or the "French French" as they're sometimes referred to. Until recently, French-Canadian plays were "translated" into French French for productions in France.

This double isolation creates a pretty much perfect situation for an artist: resentment and resilience; defensiveness and defiance. You can see why there's been such a strong instinctive bond with Scotland …

The things that sometimes frustrate me about French theatre – its elitism, literariness, self-obsession and general indifference to the lives of its audience – don't seem to apply in Québec. At the same time, the occasional tendency of British theatre towards anti-intellectualism, unthinking naturalism and an aspiration towards the condition of soap-opera – none of that seems to apply either.

The writers whose work I've come to know in Montreal and Québec City have a freshness, an audacity and a strangeness that never fails to fascinate me. There are so many names I'd like you to get to know: Evelyne de la Chenelière, Isabelle Hubert, Olivier Choinière, Serge Boucher, Fanny Britt, the amazing and prolific Carole Fréchette, Frédéric Blanchette, François Archambault and many others grouped around the beating heart of Québec contemporary theatre, Le Théâtre de la Licorne, whose founding artistic director Jean-Denis Leduc is the George Devine of French-Canadian theatre and one of the most inspiring people I've ever met.

I hope that translation and production of these writers will continue and, if it does, I've no doubt that UK audiences will fall under the spell of this unique blend of the familiar and the strange; at once recognisable and uncanny.

And that's a description that perfectly fits Catherine-Anne Toupin's play.

**Traverse Theatre Company**

The Traverse is Scotland's new writing theatre.

Formed in 1963 by a group of passionate theatre enthusiasts, the Traverse was founded to extend the spirit of the Edinburgh festivals throughout the year. Today, under Artistic Director Orla O'Loughlin, the Traverse nurtures emerging talent, produces award-winning new plays and offers a curated programme of the best work from the UK and beyond, spanning theatre, dance, performance, music and spoken word.

The Traverse has launched the careers of some of the UK's most celebrated writers – David Greig, David Harrower and Zinnie Harris – and continues to discover and support new voices – Stef Smith, Morna Pearson, Gary McNair and Rob Drummond.

With two custom-built and versatile theatre spaces, the Traverse's home in Edinburgh's city centre is a powerhouse of vibrant new work for, and of, our time. Every August, it holds an iconic status as the theatrical heart of the Edinburgh Festival Fringe.

Outside the theatre walls, it runs an extensive engagement programme, offering audiences of all ages and backgrounds the opportunity to explore, create and develop. Further afield, the Traverse frequently tours internationally and engages in exchanges and partnerships – most recently in Quebec, Turkey and South Korea.

*"The Traverse remains the best new writing theatre in Britain."*
**The Guardian**

For more information about the Traverse please visit:
www.traverse.co.uk

# Traverse Theatre

## The Ustinov Studio

Under the Artistic Directorship of Laurence Boswell, the Ustinov Studio has established itself as one of the leading studio theatres in the country. Our artistic policy is to create work new to British audiences, to be performed in themed seasons, with an emphasis on the international repertoire. We aim to discover important plays from the significant authors of the past and to present them alongside the outstanding authors of today.

The Ustinov Studio is one of the Theatre Royal Bath's three venues, which also include the award-winning egg Theatre and the historic Main House. The Ustinov Studio was reopened in 2008, newly designed by leading theatre architects Haworth Tompkins.

## Previous Ustinov productions, under the Artistic Directorship of Laurence Boswell:

AUTUMN 2015: *Monsieur Popular* by Eugène Marin Labiche in a new translation by Jeremy Sams and *The One That Got Away* by Georges Feydeau, translated by Kenneth McLeish.

SPRING 2015: *The Harvest* by Pavel Pryazhko translated by Sasha Dugdale, *Outside Mullingar* by John Patrick Shanley, *The Mother* by Florian Zeller in a new translation by Christopher Hampton.

AUTUMN 2014: *Play Strindberg* by Friedrich Dürrenmatt in a new translation by Alistair Beaton, *The Father* by Florian Zeller in a new translation by Christopher Hampton, *Exit the King* by Eugène Ionesco in a new translation by Jeremy Sams.

SPRING 2014: *The Big Meal* by Dan LeFranc, *A Steady Rain* by Keith Huff, *Intimate Apparel* by Lynn Nottage.

AUTUMN 2013: *A Lady of Little Sense* by Lope de Vega in a new translation by David Johnston, *Don Gil of the Green Breeches* by Tirso de Molina in a new translation by Sean O'Brien, *Punishment Without Revenge* by Lope de Vega in a new translation by Meredith Oakes.

SPRING 2013: *The American Plan* by Richard Greenberg, *4000 Miles* by Amy Herzog, *Fifty Words* by Michael Weller.

AUTUMN 2012: *The Welsh Boy* by Julian Mitchell adapted from *The True Anti-Pamela* by James Parry, *deadkidsongs* adapted by Gary Sefton based on the novel by Toby Litt, *The Double* by Dostoevsky adapted by Laurence Boswell.

SPRING SEASON 2012: *Red Light Winter* by Adam Rapp, *In A Garden* by Howard Korder, *In the Next Room or the vibrator play* by Sarah Ruhl.

AUTUMN 2011: *The Phoenix of Madrid* by Calderon de la Barca in a new translation by Laurence Boswell, *Iphigenia* by Goethe in a new translation by Meredith Oakes, *The* Surprise *of Love* by Marivaux in a new translation by Mike Alfreds.

## Awards and Nominations

The Ustinov was nominated for the Empty Space … Peter Brook Award in 2012, 2013 and 2015.

*In the Next Room or the vibrator play* won Best New Play at the Theatre Awards UK 2012.

*Intimate Apparel* was nominated for two London Evening Standard Theatre Awards 2014 – the Natasha Richardson Award for Best Actress and the Nook Award for Best Play.

The Ustinov Studio was Whatsonstage.com Venue of the Year South West 2014.

The Ustinov Studio was nominated for The Stage Regional Theatre of the Year Award 2015.

*The Father* was nominated for Best New Play at the UK Theatre Awards 2015 and two London Evening Standard Awards 2015 – Best Actor and Best Play. Kenneth Cranham won the Critics' Circle Theatre Award Best Actor 2015 for his performance in *The Father*.

For further information about the Ustinov Studio, please go to:
www.theatreroyal.org.uk/ustinov

**For the Ustinov Studio:**

| | |
|---|---|
| **Artistic Director** | Laurence Boswell |
| **Administrator** | Frances Macadam |
| **Finance Administrator** | Emma Bryant |
| **Marketing Officer** | Graeme Savage |
| **Duty Front of House Managers** | Samuel Burton, Jack Opie, Laura Lewis, Sarah Luscombe, Owen Morgan, Phil Tucker |
| **Chief Studios Technician** | Lloyd Evans |
| **Assistant Studios Technician** | Phil Coote |

**For the Theatre Royal Bath:**

| | |
|---|---|
| **Director** | Danny Moar |
| **Finance Director** | Gabby Akbar |
| **General Manager** | Eugene Hibbert |
| **Theatre Administrator** | Nicky Palmer |
| **Technical Manager** | Joe Wright |
| **Marketing Manager** | Anna O'Callaghan |
| **Sales Manager** | Georgie Newland |
| **Front of House Manager** | Darren Portch |

"Laurence Boswell's inventive programming is giving Bath a new theatrical buzz". **The Observer**

# Bush Theatre
## We make theatre for London. Now.

The Bush is a world-famous home for new plays and an internationally renowned champion of playwrights. We discover, nurture and produce the best new writers from the widest range of backgrounds from our home in a distinctive corner of west London.

The Bush has won over 100 awards and developed an enviable reputation for touring its acclaimed productions nationally and internationally.

We are excited by exceptional new voices, stories and perspectives – particularly those with contemporary bite which reflect the vibrancy of British culture now.

Now located in a recently renovated library building on the Uxbridge Road in the heart of Shepherd's Bush, the theatre houses a 144-seat auditorium, rehearsal rooms and a lively café bar.

Supported by
ARTS COUNCIL
ENGLAND

hammersmith & fulham

**bushtheatre.co.uk**

"A powerhouse
of new writing"
- Sunday Times Culture

# THANK YOU
## TO OUR SUPPORTERS

The Bush Theatre would like to extend a very special thank you to the following Star Supporters, Corporate Members and Trusts & Foundations whose valuable contributions help us to nurture, develop and present some of the brightest new literary stars and theatre artists.

### LONE STAR

Eric Abraham
Gianni Alen-Buckley
Michael Alen-Buckley
Rafael & Anne-Helene Biosse Duplan
Garvin & Steffanie Brown
Siri & Rob Cope
Alice Findlay
Aditya Mittal
Miles Morland
Lady Susie Sainsbury
James & Virginia Turnbull
Mr & Mrs Anthony Whyatt

### HANDFUL OF STARS

Anonymous
Martin Bartle
Clive and Helena Butler
Clare Clark
Clyde Cooper
Zarina Funk
Lesley Hill & Russ Shaw
Simon & Katherine Johnson
Emmie Jones
Paul & Cathy Kafka
V & F Lukey
Vera Monotti Graziadei
Charlie & Polly McAndrew
Paige Nelson
Georgia Oetker
Philip & Biddy Percival
Robert Rooney
Joana & Henrik Schliemann
Philippa Seal & Philip Jones QC
The van Tulleken Family
Charlotte & Simon Warshaw

### RISING STARS

ACT IV
Nicholas Alt
Anonymous
Melanie Aram
Tessa Bamford
Christopher Bevan
Charlie Bigham
David Brooks
Maggie Burrows
Simon Burstein
Matthew Byam Shaw
Jennifer Caruso Viall
Benedetta Cassinelli
Tim & Andrea Clark
Sarah Clarke
Claude & Susie Cochin de Billy
Susie Cuff

### RISING STARS CONTINUED

Liz & Simon Dingemans
Andrew & Amanda Duncan
Catherine Faulks
Natalie Fellowes
Lady Antonia Fraser
Jack Gordon & Kate Lacy
Richard Gordon
Hugh & Sarah Grootenhuis
Thea Guest
Madeleine Hodgkin
Bea Hollond
Caroline Howlett
Ann & Ravi Joseph
Davina & Malcolm Judelson
Nicola Kerr
Sue Knox
Isabella Macpherson
Penny Marland
Liz & Luke Mayhew
Michael McCoy
Fiona McDougall
Judith Mellor
Caro Millington
Ann Montier
Mark & Anne Paterson
Lauren Prakke
Barbara Prideaux
Emily Reeve
Renske & Marion
Sarah Richards
Susie Saville Sneath
Jon & NoraLee Sedmak
John & Tita Shakeshaft
Diane Sheridan
Saleem & Alexandra Siddiqi
Brian Smith
Nick Starr
Peter Tausig
Ed Vaizey
Marina Vaizey
Francois & Arrelle von Hurter
Trish Wadley
Amanda Waggott
Sir Robert & Lady Wilson
Peter Wilson-Smith & Kat Callo
Alison Winter

### CORPORATE MEMBERS

### LEADING LIGHT

Winton Capital Management

### LIGHTBULB

The Agency (London) Ltd

### SPONSORS & SUPPORTERS

Drama Centre London
Kudos Film & TV
MAC Cosmetics
Markson Pianos
Nick Hern Books
Finlay Brewer
The Groucho Club
The Law Society
Simon Gray Award
Waitrose Community Matters
West 12 Shopping & Leisure Centre

### TRUSTS AND FOUNDATIONS

The Andrew Lloyd Webber Foundation
The Austin and Hope Pilkington Trust
BBC Performing Arts Fund
The Bruce Wake Charitable Trust
The City Bridge Trust
The Daisy Trust
The D'Oyly Carte Charitable Trust
EC&O Venues Charitable Trust
The Equity Charitable Trust
Fidelio Charitable Trust
Fidelity UK Foundation
Garfield Weston Foundation
Garrick Charitable Trust
The Gatsby Charitable Foundation
The Goldsmiths' Company
Hammersmith United Charities
The Idlewild Trust
Japan Foundation
John Lyon's Charity
The J Paul Getty Jnr Charitable Trust
The John S Cohen Foundation
The John Thaw Foundation
Land Securities
The Leche Trust
The Leverhulme Trust
The Martin Bowley Charitable Trust
The Monument Trust
Pilgrim Trust
The Portrack Charitable Trust
Royal Victoria Hall Foundation
Sita Trust
The Theatres Trust
The Thistle Trust
The Williams Charitable Trust
Western Riverside Environmental Fund
The Worshipful Company of Grocers

### PUBLIC FUNDING

---

If you are interested in finding out how to be involved, please visit the 'Support Us' section of bushtheatre.co.uk or email **development@bushtheatre.co.uk** or call **020 8743 3584**

# Bush
# Theatre

RIGHT NOW

Catherine-Anne Toupin

# RIGHT NOW

translated by Chris Campbell

OBERON BOOKS
LONDON

WWW.OBERONBOOKS.COM

First published in French in 2008 by Dramaturges Éditeurs

This translation was first published in 2016 by Oberon Books Ltd
521 Caledonian Road, London N7 9RH
Tel: +44 (0) 20 7607 3637 / Fax: +44 (0) 20 7607 3629
e-mail: info@oberonbooks.com
www.oberonbooks.com

A catalogue record for this book is available from the British Library.

PB ISBN: 9781783197255
E ISBN: 9781783197262

Cover design by Well Made

Printed, bound and converted
by CPI Group (UK) Ltd, Croydon, CR0 4YY.

# Characters

BEN

ALICE

JULIETTE

FRANÇOIS

GILLES

*Right Now* had its world premiere in French, under the title *À présent,* on January 15 2008, at the Théâtre La Licorne in Montreal. It was produced by the Théâtre de la Manufacture. The play was directed by Frédéric Blanchette.

The cast were as follows:

| | |
|---|---|
| Alice | Catherine-Anne Toupin |
| Ben | David Savard |
| Juliette | Monique Miller |
| François | Éric Bernier |
| Gilles | François Tassé |

Creative Team:

| | |
|---|---|
| Set Design | Olivier Landreville |
| Costume Design | Marc Sénecal |
| Lighting Design | André Rioux |
| Original Music & Sound Design | Yves Morin |
| Prop Design | Patricia Ruel |
| Assistant Director & Stage Manager | Marie-Hélène Dufort |

*For my parents Marie and Pierre*

*Je vous aime*

# SCENE ONE

*BEN and ALICE, a couple in their early thirties, are in their flat. A large open-plan room doubles as lounge and dining room. There's a small separate kitchen and a corridor leading to the bedrooms stage right. BEN is at the dining table; he's putting papers in his briefcase. ALICE enters from the bedroom corridor. She's in her dressing gown.*

ALICE: Have you been up long?

BEN: Mmmm

ALICE: Are you off?

BEN: It's half eleven.

ALICE: God, is it?

BEN: Did you sleep well?

ALICE: No.

BEN: You were asleep when I got in. You were asleep on the settee.

ALICE: Could be.

*BEN shuts his briefcase and heads for the front door. As he passes behind the settee he stumbles on a child's toy, which gives off a loud and discordant sound. BEN freezes on the spot. He looks down at the toy for a moment then gently picks it up. He turns to show it to ALICE.*

ALICE: I forgot to tidy it away. *(Holds out her hand.)* Here.

*Silence. They look at each other.*

ALICE: Give it here!

*BEN doesn't move. ALICE goes to him and takes the toy. She goes off down the bedroom corridor. BEN watches her go then heads for the front door. He puts his bag down and puts on his coat. A few seconds and ALICE comes back in.*

ALICE: You off right now?

BEN: I should be back round midnight.

ALICE: We haven't even seen each other.

BEN: *(Getting ready to go.)* I'll see you later.

ALICE: Fifteen minutes.

BEN: I'm going to be late.

ALICE: I just want a few minutes with you.

BEN: You should have got up earlier.

ALICE: You should have woken me.

BEN: You looked really cozy. You don't get much sleep these days. We don't. I thought it would do you good to …

ALICE: Just fifteen minutes.

*He goes and puts his arms round her. Silence.*

BEN: What are you up to today?

ALICE: Don't know.

BEN: There's the bedroom. You could maybe start to …

ALICE: To what?

*Silence.*

BEN: I have to go.

ALICE: Call me in your supper break.

BEN: I won't have time.

ALICE: Around seven … OK?

BEN: OK.

ALICE: You promise?

BEN: I'll call you.

*They kiss. BEN goes. ALICE stands still for a moment. A baby starts crying softly. She turns towards the bedroom corridor.*

ALICE: *(To herself.)* Shit!

> *ALICE doesn't move. She tries to ignore the baby but the crying gets louder and louder. After a long time, she goes off down the corridor.*
>
> *Blackout.*

## SCENE TWO

*ALICE is asleep on the settee. It's late and the room is very dark. A key turns in the lock. The door opens and BEN comes in. He sees his wife and wakes her gently.*

BEN: Alice? Alice? Come to bed.

ALICE: *(Half asleep.)* Hello.

BEN: Come on.

ALICE: You shouldn't have woken me.

BEN: I'm sorry.

ALICE: I was having a dream.

BEN: Come on. You'll be more comfortable …

> *He takes her arm to help her up.*

ALICE: Shhh … You'll wake him.

BEN: Alice …

ALICE: Mustn't make any noise.

BEN: I'm not. Up you get.

ALICE: *(Getting up, still half asleep.)* Mustn't wake him up.

BEN: We're not waking anyone up.

ALICE: Be careful.

BEN: I am … I am.

ALICE: Mmmm.

BEN: Come to bed. You're out of it.

*They head down the bedroom corridor.*

*Blackout.*

## SCENE THREE

*The next day, late morning; loud knocking on the door. ALICE goes to open it, still in her dressing gown. JULIETTE, sixty, is at the door. Outside the door we see the hallway of an old, luxurious apartment building; carpeting, wallpaper, cornices etc. Directly opposite is the half-open front door of another flat.*

JULIETTE: Good morning.

ALICE: Good morning.

JULIETTE: I live in the flat opposite. That door there. I just wanted to welcome you to the building.

ALICE: That's nice of you, but we've been here for …

JULIETTE: Are you on your own?

ALICE: Yes.

JULIETTE: You don't live on your own though?

ALICE: No.

JULIETTE: No. You have a married look about you.

ALICE: Yes.

JULIETTE: How long ago did you move in?

ALICE: Almost six months.

JULIETTE: Yes, that's right, of course. And that's why we haven't met before. We've been away six months, my husband, my son and myself. *(She steps forward to get a look round the flat.)* You seem to be well settled in.

ALICE: It's coming along.

*ALICE holds on to the door to stop JULIETTE coming in.*

JULIETTE: Have you redecorated much?

ALICE: A bit.

*JULIETTE tries to see inside again.*

JULIETTE: May I come in?

ALICE: Um … Yes, yes … Come in. *(JULIETTE comes in.)* Sorry, I'm not dressed yet …

JULIETTE: Oh, I don't mind.

*JULIETTE walks about taking a good look.*

JULIETTE: Very nice. Oh yes, very nice indeed.

ALICE: Thank you.

JULIETTE: Much nicer than before.

ALICE: Yes, when we moved in, it wasn't very …

JULIETTE: It was ghastly. You can say it. The couple who lived here, before you … No taste. Absolutely no taste. The colours …

ALICE: It was very dark.

JULIETTE: It was dark, it was heavy … Did you meet them at all?

ALICE: Who?

JULIETTE: The couple who were here, before you.

ALICE: No.

JULIETTE: Good.

ALICE: The flat was already empty when we came to view.

JULIETTE: They left in a hurry.

ALICE: The previous tenants?

JULIETTE: They seemed nice enough … to begin with … when they first moved in.

ALICE: Were they here long?

JULIETTE: Only a few months. Oh yes, they left in a hurry … Didn't say goodbye.

ALICE: Did you know them well?

JULIETTE: We used to see them fairly often, and then almost overnight … I don't know … They changed. Can I see the other rooms?

ALICE: We haven't got round to …

JULIETTE: Just a peep.

ALICE: I'd really rather not, it's all over the place.

JULIETTE: I don't mind.

ALICE: But I mind. I'll do you the tour when it's all done.

JULIETTE: As you wish. *(Pause.)* Show me your hand.

ALICE: What?

JULIETTE: Give me your hand.

ALICE: Why?

JULIETTE: The right one.

*ALICE holds her right hand out to JULIETTE. JULIETTE studies the palm.*

ALICE: Do you read palms?

JULIETTE: No.

*JULIETTE drops ALICE's hand and goes to the front door.*

ALICE: *(A bit taken aback.)* Well, thanks for dropping in, it was very kind. Perhaps we could …

*JULIETTE stops in the doorway.*

JULIETTE: *(Calling towards the open door opposite.)* François? François? *(To ALICE.)* You don't mind if I get my son in? He'll be delighted with what you've done with the flat. *(Towards the hallway.)* François? He can't hear me. François, I'm talking to you! *(To ALICE.)* He must be working. *(Shouts louder.)* François!

*FRANÇOIS, mid thirties, comes out of the door opposite and joins his mother in the hall.*

JULIETTE: Didn't you hear me?

FRANÇOIS: I heard you. I just decided not to answer.

JULIETTE: François, this is … What's your name again?

ALICE: You didn't ask.

JULIETTE: Really?

ALICE: Alice.

JULIETTE: *(Doing quick introductions.)* Alice … François. François … Alice.

ALICE: Hello.

FRANÇOIS: I've seen you in the hall.

*Silence. JULIETTE comes right back into the flat, then looks at her son who has stayed in the doorway.*

JULIETTE: Come in, come in.

FRANÇOIS: May I?

ALICE: Yes. Sorry, I'm not dressed …

FRANÇOIS: Oh, I don't mind.

*FRANÇOIS comes into the flat.*

ALICE: Will anyone else be dropping in?

JULIETTE: Not for the moment.

*FRANÇOIS and JULIETTE look around the room.*

JULIETTE: It's nice, isn't it?

FRANÇOIS: Very nice.

JULIETTE: You like it?

FRANÇOIS: A lot.

JULIETTE: Not as nice as our flat, but very pleasant nonetheless. You'd be very comfy here.

FRANÇOIS: I would.

ALICE: What?

JULIETTE: Did you do the painting yourselves?

ALICE: Er … no.

JULIETTE: It really is such a good job.

FRANÇOIS: I really like it.

JULIETTE: It'd be perfect for you.

ALICE: We've only just moved in, though. We're not going to …

JULIETTE: We're not trying to chase you out of the place.

ALICE: But you just said …

JULIETTE: Just chatting. That's all. And your husband's called Ben?

ALICE: Yes.

JULIETTE: Incredible! Isn't it, François? Incredible.

FRANÇOIS: That's what I told you, Maman.

JULIETTE: Incredible.

ALICE: Have you met him?

FRANÇOIS: We bumped into each other out in the hall.

ALICE: He didn't say.

JULIETTE: Gilles and I …

ALICE: Gilles?

FRANÇOIS: My Father.

JULIETTE: Gilles and I got back from our travels yesterday, but François has been back a while.

FRANÇOIS: Last week.

JULIETTE: He told us there was a new couple in the flat opposite … The man called Ben and the woman absolutely delightful.

*Silence. JULIETTE examines ALICE.*

ALICE: Can I get you anything?

JULIETTE: Not for me. *(Silence. JULIETTE still staring at ALICE.)* You really are very attractive. I find you very attractive.

ALICE: Thank you.

JULIETTE: Even like this … not making an effort … You're very attractive. You don't see that very often, someone who looks good when they're not even trying … And I'm not just being polite. It's genuinely what I think.

ALICE: Very kind.

JULIETTE: It's true, isn't she attractive, François?

FRANÇOIS: Very attractive.

JULIETTE: You see, I'm right.

ALICE: I didn't say you weren't.

JULIETTE: You look like me.

ALICE: Do I?

FRANÇOIS: Not entirely.

JULIETTE: When I was younger. I'll bring you a photo. *(Pause.)* Does Ben work?

ALICE: Yes.

JULIETTE: Where?

ALICE: In a hospital.

JULIETTE: A doctor?

ALICE: Yes.

JULIETTE: Excellent. François could have been a doctor … François should have been a doctor, but the training …

ALICE: It's true it's a long process …

JULIETTE: It's not a question of time. It's a question of ability.

FRANÇOIS: I've never measured up to my parents' expectations.

JULIETTE: You didn't have the ability. It doesn't matter. Not every one can do it.

FRANÇOIS: I have virtually no abilities. I wasn't the one who inherited them.

JULIETTE: François …

FRANÇOIS: Yes, Maman?

*Silence.*

JULIETTE: *(To ALICE.)* You don't work yourself?

ALICE: I haven't found anything here yet. I'm looking.

*Silence. JULIETTE stares at ALICE*

JULIETTE: I can't get over it.

FRANÇOIS: I told you.

JULIETTE: It's astonishing!

ALICE: What's astonishing?

JULIETTE: It all is.

ALICE: The flat?

JULIETTE: Among other things. *(JULIETTE goes over to a photo of BEN.)* Is this your husband?

ALICE: Yes.

JULIETTE: He's exactly as I imagined him. Exactly!

ALICE: Ben?

JULIETTE: It's incredible!

ALICE: Have you met him before?

JULIETTE: In the picture … the resemblance …

ALICE: Resemblance?

JULIETTE: No, not resemblance. It's not that he looks like someone … But that's exactly how I imagine him. Exactly!

ALICE: Who does he look like?

JULIETTE: The picture I had in my mind.

ALICE: Of whom?

JULIETTE: Of him.

*Pause.*

ALICE: I don't understand.

FRANÇOIS: Don't worry about it. She's a demented old bat.

ALICE: What?

JULIETTE: I'm a demented old bat.

FRANÇOIS: You should go and have a little lie down, Maman.

JULIETTE: Not just yet.

FRANÇOIS: You're getting agitated. You're babbling.

JULIETTE: I'm quite calm.

FRANÇOIS: It's not good for you.

ALICE: What's going on?

FRANÇOIS: *(To JULIETTE.)* I'll join you in a few minutes. *(Pause. JULIETTE and FRANÇOIS look at each other.)* Go on.

JULIETTE: All right, all right.

FRANÇOIS: All right.

JULIETTE: *(Heading to the door.)* I'll leave you.

ALICE: Are you sure you're all right?

JULIETTE: Perfectly all right. I'm going for a little rest. See you soon, I hope.

ALICE: See you soon.

> *JULIETTE looks at FRANÇOIS one last time and crosses the hall to go into the flat opposite.*

FRANÇOIS: Sorry about my mother. She's a bit odd. She was determined to get a look at your flat today. She went on about it all morning.

ALICE: Why?

FRANÇOIS: Don't know. She's a demented old bat. She's hard to follow. Did it upset you, what she said?

ALICE: What?

FRANÇOIS: That I'd be comfy here.

ALICE: It's just that …

FRANÇOIS: It's true, I would be.

ALICE: Maybe so, but …

FRANÇOIS: I feel really at home. Funny, isn't it? It's just a vibe. That's all.

ALICE: We're not planning to …

FRANÇOIS: Don't worry. You're going to live here a long time. A very long time.

*FRANÇOIS picks up the photo of BEN.*

FRANÇOIS: *(To himself.)* Ben …

ALICE: What?

FRANÇOIS: Good-looking guy. *(Pause.)* Have you been married long?

ALICE: Three years.

FRANÇOIS: Funny, I don't know anyone who's married. Do you love your husband?

ALICE: Of course.

FRANÇOIS: Doesn't follow. Just cause you're married.

ALICE: No, but …

FRANÇOIS: But you do.

ALICE: Yes.

FRANÇOIS: That's good. *(Pause.)* I reckon I'd like being married. Yeah, I'm sure I'd like it.

*A baby cries softly. ALICE glances off down the corridor.*

FRANÇOIS: All right?

ALICE: Your Mother said you were in the middle of working.

FRANÇOIS: I work for my Father. Sort of like his private secretary … or slave … whatever. D'you like it here?

ALICE: *(Hesitantly.)* Yes.

FRANÇOIS: Doesn't look like it.

ALICE: We've been here nearly six months and I still don't know anyone.

FRANÇOIS: You know me.

ALICE: We don't know each other at all.

FRANÇOIS: We can fix that.

*The baby stops crying. Silence.*

FRANÇOIS: You look sad.

ALICE: Do I?

FRANÇOIS: Very.

*The baby starts crying again. ALICE turns towards the corridor again.*

FRANÇOIS: I can leave you in peace if you want?

ALICE: Do you live with your parents?

FRANÇOIS: For now. *(Pause.)* I'd love to meet Ben.

ALICE: I'm sure you will.

FRANÇOIS: We should organise something. What do you think?

ALICE: Could do.

FRANÇOIS: One evening this week … take some time to get to know each other properly.

ALICE: I'd have to talk to …

FRANÇOIS: Is Ben working Friday evening?

ALICE: I don't think so.

FRANÇOIS: OK, let's say Friday evening, around eight.

ALICE: Er … I suppose.

FRANÇOIS: Great. See you Friday then.

ALICE: See you Friday.

*FRANÇOIS goes to the door.*

*Blackout.*

## SCENE FOUR

*BEN and ALICE in their lounge. They're finishing preparations for the evening.*

BEN: I get what? Two free evenings a week?

ALICE: You're the one who said …

BEN: I said we should maybe do something, not throw a …

ALICE: Too late.

BEN: Not throw a party.

ALICE: It's not a party.

BEN: You should have asked me.

ALICE: I didn't even invite them, they invited themselves.

BEN: Brilliant!

ALICE: What?

BEN: These kind of people, you ask them round once and you've had it.

ALICE: You don't even know them.

BEN: I know the type.

ALICE: I didn't have a choice!

BEN: We'll never get rid of them now.

ALICE: You're never here anyway.

BEN: We'll have to move out to shake them off.

ALICE: It'll be me stuck with them, not you.

BEN: I'll have to give myself fifteen minutes extra in the morning for chat in the hall.

ALICE: They won't be out there waiting for you.

BEN: You don't know.

ALICE: Don't be ridiculous.

BEN: They might have nothing better to do.

ALICE: We're just having a little drink.

BEN: Why did they have to come back? We were fine when they were away.

ALICE: It might be quite funny … They do seem a bit odd.

BEN: Great …

*Knocking at the door.*

ALICE: Will you get that?

BEN: You go.

ALICE: I'm not ready.

*ALICE heads for the bedroom corridor.*

BEN: They're your guests. *(ALICE exits.)* Don't leave me on my own with them.

ALICE: *(From the bedroom.)* I'll be out in one minute. *(Knocking on the door again.)* Ben …

BEN: All right, all right … I'm going. Bloody hell …

*BEN goes to the door and opens it. GILLES, sixty, JULIETTE and FRANÇOIS are outside.*

GILLES: Good evening.

BEN: Evening.

GILLES: You must be Ben.

BEN: That's right.

GILLES: Gilles, very pleased to meet you. *(They shake hands.)* Juliette, my wife.

JULIETTE: Good evening.

BEN: Evening.

*BEN goes to shake hands but JULIETTE takes him by the shoulders.*

JULIETTE: May I?

BEN: Er … OK.

*She presses him to her and kisses him on both cheeks.*

JULIETTE: It's a great pleasure.

BEN: *(Rather overwhelmed.)* Er … likewise.

JULIETTE: You already know our son, François.

BEN: We bumped into each other in the hall.

JULIETTE: He told us.

BEN: Good evening.

*BEN and FRANÇOIS shake hands awkwardly.*

FRANÇOIS: Evening.

*Silence.*

BEN: Come on in. Make yourselves at home.

JULIETTE: Thank you.

*They all come in. BEN closes the door behind them. GILLES and JULIETTE look round at the room. FRANÇOIS looks at BEN.*

BEN: Alice is just … She'll be here any minute.

*Silence.*

BEN: *(Uncomfortably.)* Alice?

ALICE: *(Off.)* Just coming.

BEN: She's just coming.

*Silence. GILLES and JULIETTE still looking around.*

GILLES: You were right Juliette.

JULIETTE: Lovely, isn't it?

GILLES: You've done a really good job.

BEN: It's not actually finished.

GILLES: Even so, it's much better than before.

JULIETTE: Much better!

*Awkward silence.*

BEN: What can I get you?

GILLES: Red wine.

BEN: Fine. François?

FRANÇOIS: Same.

BEN: Madame..?

JULIETTE: Ben … call me Juliette.

BEN: Juliette, a drink?

JULIETTE: Do you have any sherry?

BEN: I think so.

JULIETTE: A small sherry would be lovely.

BEN: Coming right up.

*BEN goes to a sideboard and prepares five drinks.*

ALICE: *(Entering.)* I'm so sorry, I wasn't quite ready.

FRANÇOIS: Hello Alice.

ALICE: Hello.

GILLES: Good God you're absolutely gorgeous!

ALICE: Thank you.

GILLES: François, you didn't mention that.

JULIETTE: Isn't she marvellous?

GILLES: She's astounding.

ALICE: Oh stop …

GILLES: You're both astounding.

ALICE: It's embarrassing …

JULIETTE: They're perfect.

GILLES: Absolutely perfect.

JULIETTE: You're much better than the couple who lived here before.

FRANÇOIS: Maman!

JULIETTE: What? It's true.

GILLES: They were nice enough to start with.

BEN: Were you friends?

GILLES: Sort of.

BEN: Did you see a lot of them?

GILLES: Quite a lot.

BEN: *(To ALICE.)* Oh great! *(Or just a look.)*

    *Pause.*

GILLES: So, Alice, have you dressed up specially for us?

ALICE: No, for myself.

GILLES: Really?

JULIETTE: You know Ben's a doctor.

GILLES: You said.

BEN: What about you, Gilles?

GILLES: Medicine as well.

BEN: Really? What's your field?

GILLES: I do research mostly.

*BEN looks at GILLES for a moment.*

BEN: Hang on, you're not Gilles Gauche?

GILLES: I am.

BEN: <u>The</u> Gilles Gauche?

GILLES: Yes.

*BEN scans his shelves and takes down a book. He studies the back cover.*

BEN: Gosh, it is you.

GILLES: Rather younger.

BEN: If I'd known you lived next door …

GILLES: Well, now you know.

BEN: I really admire your work.

GILLES: I don't really work anymore.

BEN: It's true, you've rather disappeared …

GILLES: *(Interrupting him.)* I still do research … for my own pleasure and interest.

*Short silence.*

BEN: It's an honour. Alice, you never said.

ALICE: I didn't know.

BEN: Your ideas are really …

GILLES: Surprising?

BEN: Well yes, surprising, you could certainly say that …

GILLES: Am I to take that as a compliment?

BEN: Absolutely! *(Pause.)* Would you mind signing my book?

GILLES: I'd be delighted.

BEN: Have you got a pen, Alice?

ALICE: No.

BEN: I need a pen.

ALICE: On your desk.

BEN: Back in a second.

*He rushes off, book in hand. JULIETTE watches him go.*

JULIETTE: Well, what a handsome man! He really is a handsome man.

GILLES: Highly seductive.

JULIETTE: I'm seduced.

GILLES: Do you still find him seductive, Alice?

ALICE: I beg your pardon?

JULIETTE: Your husband.

ALICE: Uh … Yes.

*After a short silence, BEN rushes back in.*

BEN: I've got a pen.

JULIETTE: *(Studying BEN.)* It's incredible.

BEN: *(Holding out the book and the pen.)* Gilles.

JULIETTE: You are so handsome.

BEN: Sorry?

ALICE: Everyone thinks you're really handsome.

GILLES: Extremely handsome.

BEN: Thanks.

FRANÇOIS: Except me.

JULIETTE: Some people have no taste.

GILLES: *(Snatching the book from BEN.)* I'll take that, thank you.

BEN: Ouch!

ALICE: You all right?

BEN: *(Looking at his hand, which is bleeding.)* It's just a paper cut.

FRANÇOIS: That can really hurt.

BEN: So stupid.

GILLES: It was my fault.

BEN: It's nothing.

JULIETTE: Let me see your hand.

BEN: It's fine.

JULIETTE: *(Commandingly.)* Ben!

> *BEN jumps and holds out his hand. She takes it and studies it carefully.*

JULIETTE: What an odd cut … very deep.

GILLES: I'm sorry.

BEN: Just an accident.

JULIETTE: I'll put a plaster on it for you.

BEN: There's no need.

JULIETTE: Sit down.

> *She gets a plaster from her bag.*

BEN: Honestly, it's nothing.

JULIETTE: Sit down! *(He sits. She sits beside him.)* Suck your hand. *(He sucks his hand while she unwraps the plaster.)* Give. *(BEN holds out his hand and she puts the plaster on it.)* There.

BEN: Thanks.

> *Silence. JULIETTE and BEN look at each other for a moment then BEN glances at his wife.*

30

ALICE: I'll get the hors-d'oeuvre.

BEN: I'll help.

> *ALICE and BEN go to the kitchen. Once they're alone they look at each other, trying not to laugh.*

ALICE: I think you've got an admirer.

BEN: You're going down pretty well yourself. *(Pause.)* I never expected that.

ALICE: Me neither.

BEN: Gilles Gauche.

ALICE: Who is he?

BEN: I can't get over it … I was sure he was dead.

> *Meanwhile, JULIETTE has gone over to murmur something in GILLES's ear while he's signing the book. He listens and nods. FRANÇOIS goes over to them. JULIETTE murmurs something to him. After a moment, he also nods.*

BEN: You were right to ask them over.

> *BEN takes the plate of hors-d'oeuvre and makes to go; ALICE stops him.*

ALICE: Don't you think they're a bit odd?

BEN: Not odd …

ALICE: Oh come on …

BEN: A bit … unusual, maybe.

ALICE: They're more than unusual.

BEN: Well, I like them.

> *They head for the lounge.*
>
> *Blackout.*

## SCENE FIVE

*One hour later. GILLES, JULIETTE, ALICE, BEN and FRANÇOIS are in the lounge. They've been talking for some time and much wine has been drunk.*

JULIETTE: He was such a clumsy child.

GILLES: For a while we actually thought he wasn't normal.

JULIETTE: He couldn't stand up … kept falling over …

GILLES: We were discouraged.

JULIETTE: Parents should be full of admiration for their child, but with François …

GILLES: Quite impossible to admire him.

BEN: *(Jokingly.)* He was a bit gauche.

GILLES: I beg your pardon.

BEN: He was a bit gauche. *(Awkward pause.)* Gauche, it's your name and … you said he was clumsy … a bit gauche …

*After a long silence, JULIETTE shrieks with laughter. BEN and ALICE look at each other and force an embarrassed smile.*

JULIETTE: Ben, you are amazing! That is brilliant! *(She laughs for a long time.)* Oh, I haven't laughed like that for ages. No one but Benny made me laugh like that.

BEN: What, me?

JULIETTE: No, Benny.

ALICE: Who's Benny?

JULIETTE: François's brother.

ALICE: You have a brother?

FRANÇOIS: Not any more.

GILLES: François had a younger brother. He passed on, a long time ago.

FRANÇOIS: He was just a baby.

JULIETTE: *(To BEN.)* He'd be your age now.

GILLES: Yes … We've never been able to understand why *he* died.

JULIETTE: Never.

FRANÇOIS: Some mistake, I suppose.

JULIETTE: Why him?

FRANÇOIS: I mean, say if I'd died, you'd have been upset … It would have been tough for a while, but you'd have got over it.

GILLES: Parents are supposed to have a special fondness for their firstborn …

JULIIETTE: But in this case …

FRANÇOIS: It's not that you didn't love me …

JULIETTE: Not at all!

FRANÇOIS: But it must have been something about the way I cried … ate … looked at you. Everything I did was off-putting. But with Benny … even when he threw a fit it was sweet.

JULIETTE: A quite extraordinary child.

*A baby's voice can be heard offstage for a few moments. ALICE glances quickly towards the corridor.*

FRANÇOIS: Be honest, Papa.

GILLES: I don't like you calling me that.

FRANÇOIS: If you'd been given the choice. If someone had come along and asked you which of your two sons you'd rather keep … I don't think you'd have hesitated. Maman, would you have hesitated?

*Pause.*

GILLES: *(To ALICE and BEN.)* These things can't be explained. One just has preferences.

JULIETTE: *(To ALICE and BEN.)* We loved Benny more.

*Baby's voice again. ALICE turns towards the corridor. BEN watches her.*

BEN: Alice?

ALICE: Hmmmm?

BEN: Not tonight.

*The baby starts crying softly. ALICE tries to ignore it but the crying gets louder and she finds it more and more difficult.*

GILLES: But life is strange that way. I suppose it was some kind of punishment to take away the one we wanted to keep.

FRANÇOIS: Or a joke.

GILLES: A bad joke.

BEN: *(Seeing ALICE's unease.)* Alice …

ALICE: I'm all right.

JULIETTE: Would you like to see Benny?

GILLES: We've piles of photos in the flat.

JULIETTE: Photos everywhere.

FRANÇOIS: All of Benny.

ALICE: None of you?

FRANÇOIS: No.

BEN: None at all?

JULIETTE: We're sick of the sight of him already. The last thing we need is photos …

*The baby keeps crying. ALICE glances up the corridor.*

ALICE: *(Getting up.)* Excuse me.

BEN: *(Trying to keep the conversation discreet.)* Where are you going?

ALICE: I'll be right back.

BEN: Don't go.

ALICE: I won't be a moment.

BEN: I can go if you like.

ALICE: *(Sitting down again.)* No, it's fine. Forget it.

> The baby's crying gets louder and louder.

BEN: *(Aside to ALICE.)* Don't start.

ALICE: I've said, it's alright.

BEN: Everything's OK.

ALICE: I know. *(Pause. ALICE gets up.)* I'll be back.

BEN: Will you …

ALICE: I'll just be a minute.

BEN: We have guests.

ALICE: Excuse me. I won't be long.

> She goes off down the corridor. Pause.

FRANÇOIS: How long have you known each other?

BEN: Seven years.

FRANÇOIS: Long time.

JULIETTE: Do you still love each other?

BEN: Yes.

> Pause. The baby stops crying.

GILLES: Are the two of you on your own here? I mean, does your family live …

BEN: I don't really have any family. Apart from Alice.

JULIETTE: Really?

BEN: I lost my parents when I was very young.

FRANÇOIS: *(Sarcastically.)* How sad.

JULIETTE: You must feel terribly lonely.

GILLES: Ben, have you ever thought about what your life would be like without …

*ALICE enters during this line.*

BEN: Alright?

ALICE: Yes.

BEN: Sorry, Gilles, I didn't catch that.

GILLES: Doesn't matter at all.

ALICE: What were you talking about?

GILLES: Nothing. I'd very much like another drop of wine. Alice, will you join me?

ALICE: Why not.

GILLES: *(Looking round.)* Now, where are our glasses?

ALICE: No idea.

JULIETTE: There are two empties here. Whose are these?

FRANÇOIS: I think one of them's mine.

GILLES: May I?

FRANÇOIS: *(To ALICE.)* You don't mind drinking from my glass?

ALICE: No.

GILLES: *(Indicating the other glass.)* Whose is the other? No one?

ALICE: It might be mine.

GILLES: Maybe. *(He fills the two glasses.)* Which would you like?

ALICE: Doesn't matter. They're both the same.

GILLES: Not entirely.

FRANÇOIS: *(To ALICE.)* I've drunk out of one of them.

GILLES: *(To ALICE:* And you drank from the other.

ALICE: But, we don't know which is which.

FRANÇOIS: Have you a preference?

ALICE: A preference?

FRANÇOIS: Would you rather drink from your glass or from mine?

ALICE: It really doesn't matter.

GILLES: You have no preference?

ALICE: No.

GILLES: There's always a preference, even in the smallest things.

FRANÇOIS: Which one do you want?

ALICE: I'll have the one with more in.

GILLES: They're pretty much even.

ALICE: I think there's a bit more in the one on the left.

GILLES: I don't think so.

ALICE: Maybe not.

FRANÇOIS: If I tell you that one's mine, do you still want it?

ALICE: Is it yours?

FRANÇOIS: I don't know. I'm just asking if you'd still want it.

ALICE: Why not.

BEN: Looks like a bit of lipstick on the one on the right. That must be yours.

ALICE: Is there?

GILLES: There is indeed a faint trace of lipstick.

ALICE: That must be my glass.

GILLES: But you still prefer the one on the left.

ALICE: I prefer the one on the left but I'll take mine.

*GILLES holds out the right-hand glass to her.*

GILLES: *(To FRANÇOIS.)* I don't fancy drinking out of your glass.

ALICE: Would you rather have mine?

GILLES: Much rather, yes.

*ALICE offers her glass to GILLES who hands her his in exchange.*

ALICE: Thank you.

FRANÇOIS: *(To ALICE.)* You should be thanking me.

ALICE: Why?

FRANÇOIS: That's my glass. The one you wanted.

GILLES: There's always a preference, even in the smallest things.

*Blackout.*

## SCENE SIX

*BEN sits on the settee on his own, lost in thought. ALICE comes in from the bedroom. She comes over to BEN.*

ALICE: What are you thinking? *(Silence.)* Ben? *(Louder.)* Ben?

*He turns to her and looks at her vaguely, as if not quite recognising her.*

ALICE: Ben, are you alright?

BEN: Sorry … I don't know where I was.

ALICE: What were you thinking?

BEN: I've no idea.

ALICE: I'm going to bed. You coming?

BEN: In a while.

*ALICE kisses him gently.*

BEN: You were a bit of a hit tonight.

ALICE: So were you.

BEN: François was looking at you all night.

ALICE: Was he? I didn't notice.

BEN: Liar.

ALICE: Gilles looked at me a lot, but not François.

BEN: You seemed to like it.

ALICE: Do you mind?

BEN: No.

ALICE: Even if someone came on to me?

BEN: Did they?

ALICE: Maybe …

BEN: I don't believe you.

ALICE: Do you mind?

BEN: No.

*ALICE kisses him again more passionately. BEN kisses her back briefly but then gently pushes her away.*

BEN: Goodnight.

*BEN turns away and is lost in thought again. ALICE goes to the stereo and puts on some slow music. She sways softly to the sound. She turns toward BEN but he doesn't look at her. She turns up the music, goes over to BEN and dances sensuously. BEN doesn't even seem to know she's there. In a panic, ALICE turns the music up even louder. She comes right up to BEN and brushes against him with her mouth, her breasts, her hips. BEN turns to her, gazes blankly at her, then gets up and leaves the room. ALICE watches him go without moving.*

## SCENE SEVEN

*The front door is open. ALICE stands in the middle of the flat. FRANÇOIS leans against the door-frame. The room is a bit of a mess; things are all over the place.*

ALICE: You're sure you won't come in?

FRANÇOIS: I'm good here. *(Pause.)* Been out today?

ALICE: I don't go out much.

FRANÇOIS: Me neither. Specially if it's raining. I like my comforts.

ALICE: *(Indicating the mess.)* Look, sorry, I should really …

FRANÇOIS: Just tell me if I'm in the way.

ALICE: Not at all.

*ALICE starts picking a few things up.*

FRANÇOIS: I was born here, in the same flat I live in now.

ALICE: You must know everyone in the building.

FRANÇOIS: No. *(Pause.)* I really have spent too much time in my parents' flat. Just being here, round at your place, gives me the feeling I'm somewhere else.

*FRANÇOIS sees the child's toy behind the settee. He comes into the flat and picks it up. ALICE has her back turned tidying something away and doesn't see him. FRANÇOIS looks at the toy for a moment then squeezes it hard. The toy makes a loud, rather discordant sound. ALICE jumps and springs round, staring at him. FRANÇOIS starts squeezing the toy repeatedly.*

ALICE: Stop it, François! It's loud.

FRANÇOIS: I had one like that when I was a kid, but my parents confiscated it after … Where did you get it?

ALICE: It was a present. *(ALICE grabs the toy from FRANÇOIS.)* Ben doesn't like it lying about the place.

*The baby starts crying softly. ALICE turns towards the sound.*

ALICE: *(To herself.)* Shit!

FRANÇOIS: I'd better get back in the doorway.

ALICE: Uh … Could you just excuse me a sec …

*ALICE goes towards the corridor but stops halfway.*

ALICE: No, actually, it's OK. I've just remembered … It doesn't matter. What were you saying?

FRANÇOIS: Nothing.

*Pause.*

ALICE: Sorry, I'm a bit tired. I'm not sleeping much at the moment.

*The baby cries louder and louder. ALICE tries to ignore it but can't.*

FRANÇOIS: Maybe I'd better leave you to it.

ALICE: No.

FRANÇOIS: I feel a bit in the way.

ALICE: No, it's not you. It's just that … It had calmed down. It's not been a problem for months … and I don't know what's happened but now it just doesn't stop. It's getting unbearable.

FRANÇOIS: What are you talking about?

ALICE: I'm not making any sense. I'm sorry. You must think I'm nuts … But for months now it's not been … all right. Just give me a minute. I'll be back.

*She heads off again then stops again and turns back.*

ALICE: *(To herself.)* No, it's fine. It's nothing. I'm just going to leave it, that's all there is to it.

FRANÇOIS: You talking to yourself?

ALICE: Hm?

FRANÇOIS: I do that. It decorates the silence.

*FRANÇOIS goes to ALICE and tentatively tries to comfort her.*

ALICE: No, it's nothing … It's just it had stopped. I was sure it was over with but it's starting up again.

FRANÇOIS: *(Looking her straight in the eye.)* No one should ever be left on their own. When people are left on their own, that's when bad things happen.

*FRANÇOIS and ALICE are still; looking at each other.*

FRANÇOIS: My parents left me on my own one time. Big mistake.

*ALICE seems lost in FRANÇOIS's gaze. The baby's crying gets louder but it's not just from the bedroom but also from outside; from the Gauches' flat. We hear the discordant sound of the same toy, but very loud, as if someone was hitting the child with it. ALICE goes slowly towards FRANÇOIS as if to kiss him.*

*The baby stops crying.*

ALICE: *(Moving away.)* I'm sorry. I don't know why …

FRANÇOIS: You were thinking …

ALICE: I wasn't thinking anything … I was thinking … I don't know … I don't know what I was thinking.

FRANÇOIS: It's nothing.

ALICE: No, no, obviously. It's … It's … Sorry. I don't know what happened there.

FRANÇOIS: Doesn't matter.

*Brief pause.*

ALICE: Could you go.

*Blackout.*

## SCENE EIGHT

*BEN sitting on the settee. GILLES and JULIETTE sit either side of him.*

BEN: Alice always leaves something lying around … Always, somewhere about the place in here. I'll trip over a toy or … I tell her to get a grip, put everything away, but … It's as if she does it on purpose. As if she doesn't want me to put it out of my mind. Ever. She wants me to think about it all the time … So I'll be as miserable as she is. It's unbearable. I can't stand it …

GILLES: You have to be patient.

BEN: I am, but if this carries on … Sorry, I'm talking rubbish … I shouldn't be telling you this.

JULIETTE: Nonsense, of course you should.

BEN: But I just thought you'd understand. You do understand?

GILLES: We do understand.

JULIETTE: It'll all work out.

BEN: I don't see how we're going to …

GILLES: Trust us.

JULIETTE: You'll get what you want.

GILLES: Both of you.

BEN: What do you mean?

JULIETTE: You know, Ben, you know …

BEN: What I want?

JULIETTE: It'll all work out.

*BEN looks at them for a moment. ALICE comes in from the bedroom.*

ALICE: I didn't know you were here.

JULIETTE: *(Going to her.)* Oh, poor Alice.

ALICE: You should have woken me.

JULIETTE: Ben's told us everything.

ALICE: Eh?

BEN: About the baby.

GILLES: We are so sorry.

JULIETTE: Why didn't you say something?

ALICE: I didn't want to spoil the evening.

GILLES: We'd never have talked about Benny if we'd known.

JULIETTE: Never.

ALICE: You couldn't have known.

JULIETTE: Did it happen here?

BEN: We'd just moved.

GILLES: During the night?

ALICE: No, in the day.

BEN: Alice was on her own …

ALICE: He was crying …

BEN: He was always crying

JULIETTE: Then everything went quiet?

ALICE: Yes. That's right.

    *Short silence.*

ALICE: I thought he was asleep.

BEN: I found him when I got in from the hospital.

JULIETTE: How awful!

GILLES: We're here for you.

JULIETTE: *(To ALICE.)* It's not just chance that you've moved in opposite us.

ALICE: Maybe.

JULIETTE: Nothing is just chance.

ALICE: You think?

JULIETTE: I know.

BEN: They're right, Alice.

GILLES: We'll look after you.

JULIETTE: Do you want another child?

BEN: We really haven't …

JULIETTE: *(To ALICE.)* You'll have another.

GILLES: *(To ALICE.)* Soon.

JULIETTE: Very soon.

ALICE: Maybe.

JULIETTE: Of course you will.

> *Pause.*

GILLES: We'll leave you in peace.

JULIETTE: We wouldn't dream of imposing.

BEN: See you tomorrow evening.

JULIETTE: See you tomorrow, Ben, dear.

> *GILLES and JULIETTE leave.*

ALICE: Have you asked them round?

BEN: Yes.

ALICE: Again?

BEN: Do you mind?

ALICE: Just them, or..?

BEN: François as well.

ALICE: Don't you think they're a bit …

BEN: A bit what?

ALICE: I don't know.

BEN: They really like us.

ALICE: It's just …

BEN: They want the best for us.

ALICE: Sure.

> *Silence.*

BEN: I want what's best for us too, you know.

ALICE: I know.

BEN: I'm just saying … just so you know.

> *Blackout.*

## SCENE NINE

*GILLES, JULIETTE, FRANÇOIS, and BEN are sitting in the lounge. They've just finished dinner and plenty's been drunk.*

JULIETTE: Was it love at first sight?

BEN: For me it was.

GILLES: Really?

FRANÇOIS: Not for her though?

BEN: Alice was with someone.

FRANÇOIS: Could still be love at first sight.

BEN: She was with him that night.

GILLES: The night you met?

BEN: Yes.

    *ALICE comes in.*

GILLES: *(To ALICE.)* Love at first sight that night, was it?

ALICE: What?

BEN: The night we met. Alice was with her ex. He never left her side for a moment. I watched them all evening, then all of a sudden he left …

JULIETTE: Did you have a row?

ALICE: Yes.

BEN: *(To ALICE.)* When I saw you were on your own, I came straight over.

ALICE: We talked for ages.

FRANÇOIS: Did you leave together?

BEN: No, that took a lot longer. I had to really put in some work.

GILLES: You nearly missed each other.

BEN: I don't think so.

GILLES: If Alice hadn't had that row, you'd never have met.

BEN: Oh, I'd have found some way to get at her.

JULIETTE: You think?

BEN: I'm sure.

GILLES: Alice, have you ever thought what your life would be like without Ben?

ALICE: No.

GILLES: Never?

ALICE: Not really, but …

GILLES: But what?

ALICE: I suppose I'd be with someone else.

GILLES: And you'd be happy?

ALICE: I don't know … bit of an odd question.

FRANÇOIS: Not really.

GILLES: Do you think about that life at all?

ALICE: What life?

GILLES: The life you'd have if you'd not married. If you'd just carried on talking one night, rather than going quiet.

ALICE: Why do you say …

GILLES: If you'd felt nothing the first time he kissed you.

ALICE: That's not what …

GILLES: If you'd turned down the first date. If he'd never come over and talked to you. If you'd never met. If you had another life.

BEN: Everyone thinks about that sort of thing now and again.

FRANÇOIS: Do you, Alice?

ALICE: Yes.

JULIETTE: And Ben? Do you dream of a different life?

BEN: Occasionally.

*Awkward silence.*

BEN: *(To JULIETTE.)* Do you remember the first time you met?

JULIETTE: As if it was yesterday.

ALICE: Was it romantic?

JULIETTE: Was it romantic?

GILLES: Not really.

ALICE: So how was it?

JULIETTE: It was more erotic.

BEN: Erotic?

FRANÇOIS: My mother's a real tart.

GILLES: If your mother was a tart there might be just a chance that you weren't my son. No such luck, alas.

JULIETTE: I'm not a tart by any means, but I have certain tendencies …

ALICE: Tendencies?

FRANÇOIS: You'd have been a terrific tart.

JULIETTE: I had certain tendencies … Not anymore. Apart from my lingerie.

FRANÇOIS: Oh, tell us about your lingerie, Maman.

JULIETTE: I wear very colourful lingerie.

ALICE: Why?

JULIETTE: Eye-catching.

GILLES: Something purple and lacy on a white thigh; that's eye-catching.

JULIETTE: I've always liked to sit with my legs … slightly apart.

GILLES: That's how we met.

JULIETTE: It was at college. I was sitting on a wall at the top of some steps. It was hot, towards the end of summer. I had my legs just fractionally apart, but I knew that everyone coming up the steps could see that flash of purple. Everyone could see but no one said a word. I just felt their glances creeping between my legs. It was only really the men who looked … even though there were just as many women climbing the steps.

GILLES: What about you, Alice, would you have looked?

ALICE: Maybe.

FRANÇOIS: I'm sure you would have.

ALICE: I would have.

JULIETTE: You'd have been the only girl. The others didn't notice what was going on.

BEN: Or pretended not to.

GILLES: You weren't a tart, but you weren't far off.

JULIETTE: I wasn't far off.

GILLES: I'll never forget that sliver of purple.

JULIETTE: I spent the afternoon at the top of those steps …

GILLES: About two, I climbed up and spoke to you. And I wasn't really one for talking to girls I didn't know, but I was sort of … inspired.

JULIETTE: It was meant –We were meant to meet.

GILLES: Yes.

JULIETTE: We chatted for a while, then you suggested we bunk off.

GILLES: First time in my life I'd ever done it.

JULIETTE: We left the college … We walked for hours …

GILLES: Though we didn't have much to say.

JULIETTE: Later in the evening, we went to the pictures. It was a bad film, do you remember?

GILLES: Not a thing. I wasn't paying attention. I spent two hours staring at you in the dark out of the corner of my eye. The sleeve of your dress had slipped off your shoulder and I could see your bra-strap.

JULIETTE: I did that on purpose.

GILLES: We left the cinema. We walked back to college, back to the wall we'd met by earlier. You sat back down on it. You parted your legs to let me get closer to you. I ran my hand through your hair … I ran it down the length of your body … Then I put my hands on your thighs and I kissed you … *(Pause.)* A perfect moment. The kind of moment you spend your whole life trying to recapture … *(Pause.)* But time goes by and little by little the moment fades … getting fainter and fainter. Until you don't know what you're doing together at all.

*Silence.*

JULIETTE: And since that day, I buy new purple lingerie every month.

GILLES: And very sweet it is.

JULIETTE: Very.

GILLES: But cute underwear on a flabby thigh just isn't the same.

ALICE: Is it always purple?

JULIETTE: I do like purple, but I have all sorts of colours.

FRANÇOIS: And what colour are your pants this evening, Maman?

JULIETTE: I'm not saying … you'd have to take a peek.

BEN: We've no steps.

FRANÇOIS: You can't show us.

GILLES: No need for steps.

JULIETTE: It just needs someone to bend down a bit.

FRANÇOIS: Papa.

GILLES: Oh no, I've no interest these days.

ALICE: Go on …

GILLES: No.

ALICE: Why?

GILLES: I've been there too often.

FRANÇOIS: We really want to know.

BEN: Purple I bet.

JULIETTE: Maybe, maybe not.

ALICE: Whisper in my ear.

JULIETTE: No.

ALICE: I won't tell.

JULIETTE: Out of the question.

BEN: We want to know.

FRANÇOIS: The suspense is unbearable.

JULIETTE: Someone has to come and look.

FRANÇOIS: It can't be me – bad taste.

JULIETTE: Ben?

BEN: Yes?

JULIETTE: You're the lucky winner.

BEN: What?

FRANÇOIS: Go on. Get your nose between my mother's thighs.

BEN: Oh look …

GILLES: You have my permission.

BEN: It's not a question of permission.

FRANÇOIS: You're a doctor. You see this kind of thing every day.

ALICE: Go on!

BEN: No but …

ALICE: Ben.

BEN: This is mad!

JULIETTE: For me.

BEN: I can't do it.

GILLES: You wanted to know a minute ago.

BEN: Yes, but I thought it'd be you who …

ALICE: Go on.

BEN: I can't put …

ALICE: Go on!

JULIETTE: Come on.

BEN: No.

FRANÇOIS: But we really want to know.

BEN: Lift your leg up a bit and we can all have a look.

JULIETTE: At my age?

BEN: If you could just …

JULIETTE: No! Someone has to get down on the floor. My leg lifting days are over.

*Short pause.*

FRANÇOIS: Go on, on your knees.

BEN: Eh?

ALICE: Get on your hands and knees.

BEN: Alice …

ALICE: It's just a laugh.

JULIETTE: For my sake.

BEN: This doesn't seem right.

GILLES: On you go, Ben.

BEN: I can't …

FRANÇOIS: On your knees, on your knees, on your knees …

*FRANÇOIS chants. ALICE, GILLES, and JULIETTE join in.*

FRANÇOIS, ALICE, GILLES, JULIETTE: On your knees, on your knees, on your knees …

BEN: Ok, ok … I'm doing it..

*BEN stands in front of JULIETTE. He hesitates, then gets down on his hands and knees. He ducks his head and tries to look up her skirt.*

BEN: Can't see a thing.

JULIETTE: Come closer.

*BEN crawls towards her.*

JULIETTE: Closer.

*BEN crawls a bit closer.*

JULIETTE: Closer.

*BEN crawls right up to her, his nose against her knees. He looks up at her.*

JULIETTE: Go on, Ben.

*Awkwardly, BEN tries to put his head under her skirt.*

BEN: Uh … I can't see anything. Your legs are stuck together.

JULIETTE: I'm playing hard to get.

BEN: *(Jumping to his feet.)* No, this is mad!

JULIETTE: Down!

*He gets down again at once.*

JULIETTE: Ready?

BEN: I think so.

JULIETTE: Because I won't keep my legs apart very long.

FRANÇOIS: Thank Christ.

BEN: Ready.

*JULIETTE lifts her skirt a little and parts her legs slightly. After a beat, BEN puts his head under her skirt.*

ALICE: Can you see anything?

BEN: It's a bit dark in here.

FRANÇOIS: Lift your skirt a bit more, Maman.

*JULIETTE does so.*

JULIETTE: Like that?

BEN: Uh … yes.

ALICE: Can you see?

BEN: They're … purple … No, hang on, not purple … I'd say fuchsia. They're fuchsia.

FRANÇOIS: Fuchsia?

ALICE: That's original.

*BEN takes his head out from under JULIETTE's skirt and looks at her.*

BEN: I'd say that's fuchsia.

JULIETTE: A discerning eye.

*JULIETTE pulls down her skirt and BEN stands up. ALICE goes to the stereo to put a CD on.*

FRANÇOIS: Filthy job, but …

GILLES: Thank you, Ben.

BEN: Not at all.

JULIETTE: Most enjoyable.

BEN: I'm glad.

JULIETTE: Was it enjoyable for you as well?

BEN: Uh … Yes. Strange, but … enjoyable.

*Pause. Slow, soft music from the stereo.*

GILLES: Oh good idea!

ALICE: I felt like …

GILLES: *(Looking into ALICE's eyes.)* You are marvellous.

ALICE: Should we open another bottle, Ben?

GILLES: Dance with me.

ALICE: Now?

GILLES: That's why you put the music on; so someone would ask you. Am I right?

ALICE: No.

GILLES: I feel like dancing.

ALICE: Later maybe.

GILLES: I'm going to insist. Is that what you're after? Don't you play too hard to get, now. *(He puts his arm around ALICE's waist. She's slightly uncomfortable.)* Do you mind?

ALICE: No.

GILLES: Ben, you don't mind if I dance with Alice?

BEN: Not at all.

GILLES: Resistance is useless … *(He presses her against him and looks into her eyes.)* I'm sure you'd rather dance with someone else but there's no choice; it has to be me … Ben barely sees you anymore, he takes you for granted … and my son is too dense to notice a beautiful woman. *(They dance.)* You know, Alice, I used to love my wife so much. But not anymore.

JULIETTE: Mad with love.

GILLES: I adored you. But not anymore.

JULIETTE: I know.

GILLES: I don't desire her at all anymore.

JULIETTE: Not at all.

GILLES: But it may be, tonight, when we go to bed, it may be that I'll turn to her, kiss her, make love to her … it's possible … But, of course, I wouldn't be with her. I'd be with you, Alice. I'd be thinking of you. Making love to you, Alice, not my wife. *(Pause.)* Nothing lasts.

JULIETTE: What about you, Ben? When you lie down beside Alice tonight … will you want to make love?

GILLES: I doubt it.

JULIETTE: Me too.

BEN: What?

GILLES: They haven't made love in weeks.

ALICE: That's not true.

GILLES: Yes it is. It's written all over you, Alice … everything you do … the need to be … wanted.

ALICE: Rubbish.

GILLES: I don't think so.

*Pause. GILLES and ALICE still dancing.*

JULIETTE: We'd better give them a prod.

GILLES: If you want another baby …

JULIETTE: Come and dance, Ben.

BEN: No really …

*JULIETTE drags him to her. She presses against him and they dance.*

JULIETTE: It's been much too long.

GILLES: It's been months.

JULIETTE: Such a shame.

BEN: But it's none of your business.

JULIETTE: Ben, I'm sure Alice is as beautiful today as the day you met.

BEN: Yes.

GILLES: Probably more beautiful.

JULIETTE: Yet you feel nothing … no desire any more … no attraction …

GILLES: Nothing.

JULIETTE: Am I wrong?

*Pause.*

GILLES: He's not even arguing.

BEN: Alice knows I love her.

JULIETTE: Will you want her tonight?

BEN: That's not the sort of thing you can …

GILLES: I want her.

BEN: … say in advance.

JULIETTE: I'm simply asking if you'll want her tonight.

GILLES: When Alice steps out of the shower, hair all wet, skin all glistening … Do you still find her desirable?

JULIETTE: When she slips on her underwear in the morning, before she gets dressed … do you still want to take them off … tear them off?

GILLES: Do you wear nice underwear? *(He's looking right at her and she can't reply.)* I'm sure you do.

*GILLES gently slips the sleeve of ALICE's dress off her shoulder so her bra strap can be seen. He stops dancing to concentrate on ALICE's shoulder.*

JULIETTE: Say you do make love to your wife tonight, Ben. Who will you be thinking about?

BEN: About her.

GILLES: Do you believe that Alice?

ALICE: *(Her eyes fixed on GILLES.)* Maybe.

JULIETTE: Who will you be thinking about?

BEN: No one.

JULIETTE: Will it be me?

BEN: Uh …

JULIETTE: Will you be on all fours between my legs? Is that what'll inspire you? Will it be me who inspires you?

FRANÇOIS: That would inspire me all right.

*Pause. ALICE and BEN each seem hypnotised by their partners.*

JULIETTE: Well, Ben?

BEN: …

JULIETTE: Answer me.

BEN: No, I …

JULIETTE: You can tell me everything.

BEN: Yes.

JULIETTE: I already know everything about you, Ben.

BEN: Do you?

JULIETTE: You can't keep anything from me.

BEN: No.

JULIETTE: You can't keep anything from me, not any more.

*The two couples dance very close. GILLES and JULIETTE are about to kiss their partners. FRANÇOIS gets up and goes over to GILLES.*

FRANÇOIS: You should give me a go with Alice.

GILLES: Not now.

FRANÇOIS: It's my turn.

GILLES: Leave us in peace.

FRANÇOIS: But I'd have liked …

JULIETTE: Later, François.

*Pause.*

FRANÇOIS: Maman, Papa ….

GILLES: Sit down.

FRANÇOIS: Far be it from me to interfere …

JULIETTE: You'll get your turn.

FRANÇOIS: … but if you don't want Alice and Ben to get the wrong idea …

GILLES: Leave us be.

FRANÇOIS: … you should lay off a bit.

JULIETTE: It won't be long.

GILLES: Just a second …

*GILLES and JULIETTE kiss ALICE and BEN. After a few seconds the CD jams. BEN and ALICE come to with a start and break away from GILLES and JULIETTE. ALICE rushes over to stop the music. Silence.*

GILLES: Thank you, Alice.

*Silence.*

JULIETTE: *(To ALICE.)* Gilles is such a good dancer. *(Pause.)* Am I a good dancer, Ben?

*Silence.*

ALICE: I'll tidy up a bit.

*ALICE collects some plates from the table and heads for the kitchen.*

GILLES: I'll give you a hand.

ALICE: It's all right.

GILLES: I insist.

*GILLES picks up some cutlery and joins ALICE in the kitchen.*

ALICE: Leave those on the side, I'll take care of them.
*(GILLES does so.)* Thanks.

*GILLES stares at ALICE as she goes about things in the kitchen.*

GILLES: You can say it now.

ALICE: *(Turning to him.)* Hmm?

GILLES: I'm here.

ALICE: Sorry?

GILLES: I'm listening.

ALICE: Listening?

GILLES: You wanted to tell me something.

ALICE: No.

*Pause.*

GILLES: What were you wanting to tell me?

ALICE: Nothing.

GILLES: You can tell me anything at all, you know.

BEN: *(Calling from the lounge.)* Alice, d'you need a hand?

JULIETTE: Gilles is taking care of it.

ALICE: It's fine.

*JULIETTE sits on the settee in the lounge.*

GILLES: You're nervous.

ALICE: What makes you say that?

GILLES: Your heart is thumping.

ALICE: I don't think it is.

GILLES: Do I make you nervous?

ALICE: No.

GILLES: You mustn't be.

> *Note: To make these simultaneous scenes easier to read, the lines on the left refer to action in the kitchen; those on the right to the lounge.*

JULIETTE: Let me see your hand.

BEN: Why?

JULIETTE: The cut.

BEN: It was nothing.

JULIETTE: Give me your hand.

*BEN holds his hand and JULIETTE looks at it.*

GILLES: I can go if you like.

ALICE: It's not that.

GILLES: You don't want me to go?

ALICE: No, I mean, if I seem nervous it's not because of you. It's not you. It's …

GILLES: It's what?

ALICE: Nothing.

JULIETTE: It's nearly healed over.

BEN: It was nothing serious.

*BEN tries to take his hand away. JULIETTE holds on to it.*

JULIETTE: Wait.

*BEN sits beside her.*

GILLES: Let me help you.

ALICE: It'll only take two minutes.

GILLES: I wasn't talking about the dishes.

ALICE: What were you talking about?

*ALICE and GILLES look at each other in silence.*

BEN: Do you read palms?

JULIETTE: *(Studying the hand.)* No.

GILLES: I'm listening.

ALICE: You'll think I'm mad …

GILLES: You know you're going to tell me. Why wait?

JULIETTE: It's going to leave a mark.

BEN: Just a tiny scar.

GILLES: I'm listening.

JULIETTE: You're marked for life.

ALICE: I'm here, on my own, all day. It's so silent. Sometimes I think I … I imagine … I hear things. I'm not mad but … Why am I telling you this? It's ridiculous.

GILLES: What do you hear?

ALICE: *(Turning back to the dishes.)* Nothing, nothing …

FRANÇOIS: *(To BEN.)*
You should be more careful.
Scars don't go away.

GILLES: *(Going to ALICE.)* You want to tell me. Don't be scared.

*Pause. ALICE turns back to face GILLES.*

> *FRANÇOIS rolls up his sleeves and the legs of his trousers.*

ALICE: I used to hear them a few months ago, after … It's as if it comes from somewhere else … as if I were somewhere else.

> *JULIETTE kisses BEN's hand lightly then lets it go.*

GILLES: Somewhere else where?

ALICE: Nowhere. Here, but somewhere else. At first I thought it was all right, that it would stop … And it had stopped … but now it's started again … it's not right …

GILLES: It's perfectly all right. Everything that's happening to you is perfectly natural.

ALICE: What, hearing things that aren't there?

GILLES: If you like hearing them, it's perfectly all right.

ALICE: If I like it?

> FRANÇOIS: *(Examining his elbows and knees.)* I've got scars everywhere.

> *JULIETTE strokes BEN's thigh, smiling blissfully.*

GILLES: You do like hearing these things?

ALICE: No.

GILLES: If you didn't like it you wouldn't be able to hear them. *(He looks into her eyes. Embarrassed, she turns her back.)* You must desire it, in some sense … You need it.

ALICE: But it's not right to …

GILLES: *(Getting closer still.)* There's nothing right or wrong in itself. It's all a matter of perspective.

> FRANÇOIS: Hey Ben, have you got loads?

> BEN: What?

> JULIETTE: Scars.

64

GILLES: If I put my hands on your hips … like this.
  *(He does so.)* Is that right?
  Does it worry you? Does it make you feel uncomfortable?

ALICE: Yes.

GILLES: You're not moving them though. There must be a
  sense in which you like it. Some part of you wants my
  hands on you, otherwise I wouldn't have done it. Am
  I taking advantage? I don't think so. If I were taking
  advantage you'd have gone back to the lounge long ago …
  or somewhere else.

> FRANÇOIS: Did your maman put a plaster
> on it when you hurt yourself?

> BEN: I've told you, my mother died
> when I was very young.

> JULIETTE: Do you remember her?

> BEN: All I remember is that,
> one day, she wasn't there any more.

> *JULIETTE is still stroking his thigh in a maternal way.*

GILLES: And if I just slide my hands along your body.
  *(He slides his hands round her waist.)* Is that right?
  *(ALICE lets him.)* Answer me, Alice. Is this right?

ALICE: No.

GILLES: Then stop me!

*Pause. Both stand motionless. He slowly puts his hands on her breasts.*

GILLES: Stop me! *(She doesn't move. He presses against her.)*

> JULIETTE: You're unhappy, Ben.

> BEN: No, I …

> JULIETTE: You are!

GILLES: You see, nothing's wrong in itself. It's all relative. If you like it … If you want it … why on earth would it be wrong? *(Pause.)* You hear voices … you want to … just as you want me … now, in this moment.

ALICE: I don't want anything. It's not me …

JULIETTE: So unhappy.

FRANÇOIS: Do you like your scars, Ben?

ALICE: It's not me, I just hear them.

FRANÇOIS: *(Still examining his skin.)* I love mine. I look at them for hours … There's just one I'd like to get rid of.

GILLES: You mustn't be scared. Everything is perfectly right.

*He turns ALICE to face him; takes her by the waist and lifts her to sit on the counter.*

JULIETTE: Death is following you around.

BEN: Death?

JULIETTE: To lose your family twice over …

BEN: I've still got Alice.

JULIETTE: Are you sure?

FRANÇOIS: Ben, have you got a scar you'd like to get rid of? A scar, or a person …

BEN: *(Calling to the kitchen.)* Alice, sure you're OK in there?

ALICE: *(To BEN.)* Sure, yeah.

GILLES: You don't want anyone to disturb us, do you?

ALICE: No.

*GILLES strokes ALICE's calves with his fingertips.*

JULIETTE: You needed this family so much …

BEN: *(Stands, ill at ease.)* More wine?
I'll get another bottle from the kitchen.

*BEN heads for the kitchen.*

JULIETTE: No!

BEN: What?

JULIETTE: Sit down again.

GILLES: Open your legs.

JULIETTE: There's no hurry.

BEN: I'm just getting another bottle.

JULIETTE: It can wait.

GILLES: For me.

JULIETTE: Come back here beside me.

*BEN looks at her without moving.*

GILLES: Open your legs.

ALICE: Why?

GILLES: I want to see what colour you're wearing.

ALICE: Not purple.

JULIETTE: I've just had a picture
of you as a little boy, Ben.

BEN: As a little boy?

JULIETTE: Yes, it's that way you have of looking at me …

GILLES: What colour are they?

ALICE: Black.

GILLES: Black? Are you sure?

JULIETTE: When you look at me like that
I see the little boy you used to be.
A lonely, shy little boy …

FRANÇOIS: Hey, Ben, did you ever do
anything naughty?

GILLES: I don't think you've got any on.

ALICE: What?

GILLES: Any underwear.

JULIETTE: Always so sad …

FRANÇOIS: Got anything naughty
to say sorry for?

ALICE: Oh yes I have.

FRANÇOIS: I've got loads

GILLES: Well then, let me see.

*GILLES calmly lifts ALICE's dress.*

JULIETTE: A little lost boy …
looking for his Maman.

BEN: *(Tearing his eyes off her.)* Alice?

ALICE: *(Abruptly stopping
GILLES from lifting her dress.)*
Just a sec!

JULIETTE: Ben, come here by me.

BEN: I wanted to give Alice a hand.

JULIETTE: You can't do anything for her.

GILLES: Let me see Alice …

ALICE: They're black.

GILLES: Let me see.

JULIETTE: You must have missed your Maman.

FRANÇOIS: *(To himself.)* You don't miss
what you've never had.

JULIETTE: You still miss her, don't you?

BEN: Dreadfully.

GILLES: I want to see.

ALICE: Why?

GILLES: Because you want to show me.

*GILLES kneels in front of ALICE.*

JULIET: *(To BEN.)* I miss Benny.
I've always missed him … my little lad.

GILLES: Open your legs.

*ALICE opens her legs.*

JULIETTE: I remember,
a few months after he died,
I was doing some shopping,
on my own in some big supermarket.

FRANÇOIS: No, I was there!

GILLES: Lift your dress.

*ALICE lifts her dress above her knees.*

JULIETTE: I walked up and down the aisles, not knowing what
to buy, not knowing …

FRANÇOIS: I was right behind you.

ALICE: Like that.

GILLES: Like that, yes.

*GILLES looks up her dress.*

JULIETTE: Then I found myself
in an empty aisle; no one else around.

GILLES: You weren't lying.

JULIETTE: And I noticed a trolley
in the middle of the aisle.

FRANÇOIS: I was right there behind you.

GILLES: Black and very pretty.

*ALICE closes her legs. GILLES takes hold of one of her feet, takes off
her shoe and starts to kiss her ankle gently.*

JULIETTE: The trolley was empty,
except there was a little boy sitting in the child seat.

FRANÇOIS: I was trying to grab your hand.

JULIETTE: The little boy was utterly absorbed in a toy.

BEN: Why are you telling me this?

JULIETTE: His eyes were glued to this toy.

*BEN sits beside JULIETTE.*

GILLES: Still thinking about him, Alice?

JULIETTE: Then he looked up for a moment.
Then left, then right.
Then he looked behind him.
Then left and right again.
And in front and behind …

FRANÇOIS: Hold my hand, Maman.

*GILLES continues kissing ALICE's ankle, gently lifting her calf.*

GILLES: You're wasting your time.

JULIETTE: He was so upset.
He was looking everywhere.

BEN: He was looking for someone.

GILLES: He won't come.

JULIETTE: He was looking
but there was no one there.
So he started crying,
louder and louder.

GILLES: Call him and see.

BEN: But no one came.

JULIETTE: No one.

FRANÇOIS: Hold my hand, Maman.

GILLES: *(Looking up at ALICE.)* Call him.

*GILLES calmly carries on kissing her thighs.*

JULIETTE: I wanted to hug the little fellow
and make it all better
then take him away with me.

BEN: Yes …

JULIETTE: I went over. I picked him up
and gave him a big hug.

BEN: And after that? What did you do then?

FRANÇOIS: You wanted to dump me
in the trolley instead of him,
didn't you, Maman? You wanted
to leave me there and go off with him.

*FRANÇOIS starts pacing up and down agitatedly.*

GILLES: Call him.

ALICE: No.

GILLES: Why?

*GILLES straightens and looks into her eyes.*

JULIETTE: I took a few steps,
but then I stopped.

GILLES: Why, Alice?

JULIETTE: I put the little chap down
on the floor and ran off.

*FRANÇOIS starts hunting for a book on the shelves.*

GILLES: Why don't you call him?

ALICE: I don't know.

GILLES: Because you know he won't come.

FRANÇOIS: *(Taking a book from the shelves.)*
Aha! Here it is.

JULIETTE: I should never have left like that.

FRANÇOIS: Ben, did you read
what my Father wrote in your book?

GILLES: Call him and see.

ALICE: No.

FRANÇOIS: That's really touching.

GILLES: Call him.

FRANÇOIS: Really, really touching.

JULIETTE: But I won't make that mistake again.

ALICE: *(Shouting.)* Ben!

FRANÇOIS: Really generous!

ALICE: *(Shouting.)* Ben?

GILLES: You see. He won't come now, Alice.

FRANÇOIS: I really think
everyone should hear this.

GILLES: He's a long way away.

FRANÇOIS: Dad, I know you've got
your hands full in there …

JULIETTE: *(With huge affection.)*
Oh Ben, dear little Ben …

FRANÇOIS: I'm sure you can hear me though.
So here it is: "To a most accomplished young man, of
whom I shall soon be very proud …

JULIETTE: You've been that little boy,
haven't you Ben?

FRANÇOIS: *(Still reading.)* "Affectionately … Gilles"

GILLES: *(Gently running his hand through her hair.)*
This is what you wanted Alice, isn't it?

JULIETTE: Often you've looked round desperately for
someone.

ALICE: Yes.

BEN: Often.

*GILLES runs his hand down ALICE's body.*

FRANÇOIS: *(Shutting the book.)*
That is really touching.
*(Very loudly.)* Is everyone touched?
Course they are.
You should treasure this book, Ben.

BEN: Very often.

FRANÇOIS: *(To BEN.)* It's so precious

GILLES: He can't do anything for you now.

*GILLES puts both hands on ALICE's thighs.*

FRANÇOIS: *(To BEN, who doesn't listen.)*
Don't you worry, Ben.
I'll take very good care of it.

JULIETTE: And you're still looking.

BEN: Yes …

*FRANÇOIS puts the book back on a shelf.*

JULIETTE: And you still haven't found them.

GILLES: Don't be scared.

*GILLES kisses her gently.*

FRANÇOIS: *(Drops the book on purpose.)*
Oops! What an idiot!
I am so clumsy.

JULIETTE: Still haven't found them.

BEN: No.

JULIETTE: Little lad still looking for his Maman.

*FRANÇOIS reaches for another book and knocks it off the shelf.*

FRANÇOIS: Oh no!

JULIETTE: Looking around, all frightened and lost.

FRANÇOIS: *(Knocking another book off.)*
I'm just so cack-handed …

*GILLES steps back from ALICE and looks at her.*

GILLES: Let yourself go, Alice.

JULIETTE: You're not lost any more,
little Ben. I'm here.

BEN: Are you?

GILLES: If you let yourself go you'll get what you want.

ALICE: You think?

FRANÇOIS: *(Dropping another book.)* Oops!

JULIETTE: I'm here.

*BEN is overcome.*

GILLES: I know.

JULIETTE: *(Holding out her arms.)*
My brave little boy … come here.

*BEN clings to her, sobbing gently.*

GILLES: Everything you want.

*ALICE stares at him a moment, then kisses him passionately.*

FRANÇOIS: *(Dropping another book.)*
How very gauche of me! *(Laughs.)*
Don't mind me nicking your gag,
Ben, do you? Such a cracker.
We were all just dying to hear it again.
*(Drops another book.)* Oops!

JULIETTE: You've been so hurt, haven't you?

*FRANÇOIS starts knocking all the books off the shelves
more and more aggressively. He cuts himself on one of them.*

FRANÇOIS: Ouch! *(Looks at the cut.)* Another scar!

JULIETTE: There, there, don't cry.

*GILLES and ALICE kiss more and more passionately.*

FRANÇOIS: *(Still knocking books off.)* What an idiot.
What a twat. I'm making a complete fucking shambles here.

JULIETTE: I should have taken him … I should have taken you
that day and kept you with me.

*BEN nods in agreement.*

JULIETTE: *(Tenderly.)*
I won't make the same mistake twice.

FRANÇOIS: *(Going to the stereo.)*
Could do with some music, don't you reckon?

*He puts on the same music as before.*
*After a few seconds, the CD starts jamming.*

JULIETTE: *(To BEN.)* I'm here, Ben, I'm here.

BEN: *(Being comforted.)* It's been so hard …

*BEN clings to her and she rocks him as though he were a little boy.*

FRANÇOIS: *(Jumping around to the music.)*
It's good this. I like it!

*ALICE detaches herself from GILLES for a moment. She sweeps the plates and cutlery off the kitchen counter and lies down on it.*

JULIETTE: Baby won't hurt any more.

*BEN starts sucking his thumb.*

FRANÇOIS: Maman? Papa?

*GILLES gets up and lies on top of ALICE.*

FRANÇOIS: *(Yelling.)* Look at me! Look at this!

*FRANÇOIS hurls himself headfirst onto the settee, feet in the air. He's right next to JULIETTE and BEN but they don't seem to notice him.*

FRANÇOIS: *(Waving his legs about.)*
Alice! Come and look!

JULIETTE: My baby, my baby … I've found you at last.

FRANÇOIS: Look at me!

JULIETTE: *(To BEN, softly.)* Don't cry now.

FRANÇOIS: *(Yelling towards the kitchen.)* Alice!
Come and look at me!

JULIETTE: I'm here.

BEN: *(To himself, as if dozing off.)* You're there.

JULIETTE: I'm right here, everything's all right now.

*BEN stays cradled on JULIETTE's breast, quiet and at peace.*
*FRANÇOIS hurls himself about on the settee.*
*GILLES and ALICE carry on kissing on the kitchen counter.*

*The CD is still jamming.*

*Blackout.*

## SCENE TEN

*JULIETTE and ALICE in the flat. JULIETTE is giving ALICE a present.*

JULIETTE: I thought of you the moment I saw it.

ALICE: You didn't have to.

JULIETTE: Of course I didn't have to. It's a present.

*ALICE hesitates then unwraps the present. It's a child's pyjama suit. She looks at it open-mouthed.*

JULIETTE: It's so sweet. Don't you think?

ALICE: Yes …

JULIETTE: I couldn't not buy it.

*Silence.*

ALICE: It's … It's very kind of you. I'm touched, but …

JULIETTE: Stop right there. I know what you're going to say.

ALICE: I'm … I'm not …

JULIETTE: I know. *(The sound of a baby crying softly. ALICE freezes.)* But I'm sure you will be soon.

*ALICE tries to hide her discomfort. JULIETTE watches her. The baby cries. ALICE puts the pyjama-suit back in its box.*

JULIETTE: Aren't you going to go?

ALICE: Hmm?

JULIETTE: You can go and check. I don't mind.

ALICE: What?

JULIETTE: I know what it's like. Go ahead, I'll wait here.

ALICE: I don't understand what …

JULIETTE: Go and see.

ALICE: See what?

JULIETTE: Isn't that what you usually do?

ALICE: Huh?

JULIETTE: It's what you did the other night.

    *Short pause.*

    *Pause.*

ALICE: Can you hear it?

JULIETTE: Hmm?

ALICE: Can you hear it?

JULIETTE: Yes.

ALICE: What can you hear?

JULIETTE: The same thing as you.

ALICE: You can hear it?

JULIETTE: Of course.

ALICE: That's not possible.

JULIETTE: Is it always this loud?

ALICE: You can't hear it.

JULIETTE: You should go and see.

ALICE: See what?

JULIETTE: If he's there.

ALICE: Who?

JULIETTE: You know who I'm talking about.

ALICE: What can you hear?

JULIETTE: The same as you.

ALICE: What can you hear?

*The baby stops crying abruptly. Silence. ALICE looks at JULIETTE who remains impassive.*

ALICE: What can you hear?

JULIETTE: Nothing. *(Pause.)* It's stopped.

*Blackout.*

## SCENE ELEVEN

*ALICE is asleep on the settee. It's late and the room is dark. We hear a key in the door. FRANÇOIS comes in. He comes over to ALICE on the settee. He bends over her. He's a few inches from her face when she wakes.*

ALICE: *(Half asleep.)* Hi …

FRANÇOIS: Hi.

ALICE: What time is it?

FRANÇOIS: Late.

ALICE: How's the hospital?

FRANÇOIS: It's not Ben.

ALICE: Hmm?

FRANÇOIS: It's François.

*She opens her eyes then jerks upright with a cry and rushes to switch on the light.*

ALICE: What are you doing here?

FRANÇOIS: I wanted to see you.

ALICE: Eh?

FRANÇOIS: I wanted to see you but I didn't want to wake you.

ALICE: How did you get in?

FRANÇOIS: I've got a key.

ALICE: Since when?

FRANÇOIS: Ben gave it me.

ALICE: I didn't know.

FRANÇOIS: For emergencies.

ALICE: There isn't one.

FRANÇOIS: I heard you yelling. That's why I came.

ALICE: Yelling?

FRANÇOIS: I didn't want to wake you.

ALICE: You heard me?

FRANÇOIS: You weren't supposed to wake up.

ALICE: I don't remember …

FRANÇOIS: I just wanted to make sure you were OK.

ALICE: I think I am.

FRANÇOIS: You must have had a nightmare.

ALICE: Maybe.

FRANÇOIS: I just wanted to make sure …

ALICE: I don't remember yelling.

FRANÇOIS: Just a bad dream.

ALICE: I don't remember.

FRANÇOIS: Do you remember your dreams?

ALICE: Some.

FRANÇOIS: You looked really peaceful.

ALICE: I thought I was yelling?

FRANÇOIS: But when I came in. You seemed peaceful.

ALICE: I think I was fine.

FRANÇOIS: Are you not now?

ALICE: I'm just a bit …

FRANÇOIS: Asleep?

*FRANÇOIS approaches her and looks into her eyes.*

ALICE: I think I'm going to go to bed.

FRANÇOIS: Shall I stay?

ALICE: What for?

FRANÇOIS: Just till you get to sleep. Then I'll go.

ALICE: It must be midnight.

FRANÇOI: Half past.

ALICE: Ben should be home soon.

FRANÇOIS: Really?

ALICE: Yes.

FRANÇOIS: I should stay anyway.

ALICE: There's no need.

FRANÇOIS: You sure?

ALICE: Yes.

FRANÇOIS: You don't want me to stay?

*Pause.*

FRANÇOIS: I'll stay.

ALICE: There's no need.

FRANÇOIS: No more nightmares?

ALICE: I can't control it.

FRANÇOIS: I'd be better staying.

ALICE: No.

FRANÇOIS: *(Gently but firmly.)* You want me to stay.

ALICE: No.

FRANÇOIS: I'll stay.

ALICE: You want to?

FRANÇOIS: If you want me to.

ALICE: Yes.

FRANÇOIS: I'll stay then.

ALICE: Stay.

>  *Silence. FRANÇOIS strokes ALICE's hair.*

FRANÇOIS: I knew there was something wrong.

ALICE: Something wrong?

FRANÇOIS: I was worried. I didn't want you left on your own.

>  *FRANÇOIS strokes her body.*

ALICE: What are you doing?

>  *FRANÇOIS brings his face close to hers. We hear a key in the lock. FRANÇOIS moves away quickly. BEN enters.*

BEN: François?

FRANÇOIS: *(Completely calm.)* Hi there.

BEN: Am I disturbing you?

FRANÇOIS: Not at all.

ALICE: I had a nightmare.

BEN: Again?

FRANÇOIS: Yes.

ALICE: I was yelling.

FRANÇOIS: Woke me up.

ALICE: He came to see I was OK.

FRANÇOIS: Alice isn't having a good time.

ALICE: I'm not.

FRANÇOIS: That's why I'm here.

BEN: Nice of you.

FRANÇOIS: No problem.

*Pause.*

ALICE: I didn't know you'd given him a key.

BEN: Good thing I did.

ALICE: Yes.

FRANÇOIS: Come in.

BEN: I don't want to disturb you.

FRANÇOIS: Alice needed to talk.

BEN: You need to talk?

ALICE: Must do.

BEN: Pretend I'm not here.

*BEN comes in, puts down his briefcase and takes off his coat.*

ALICE: *(To BEN.)* Are you sleepy?

BEN: Yes.

ALICE: Me too.

FRANÇOIS: *(To BEN.)* You should go to bed.

BEN: I've got work to do.

FRANÇOIS: In here?

BEN: Yes.

FRANÇOIS: We'll be in your way.

BEN: I don't think so.

FRANÇOIS: We were talking quite loud.

BEN: I'm used to noise when I'm working.

*Pause.*

FRANÇOIS: Why don't you go and work in my room?

BEN: In your parents' place?

FRANÇOIS: Perfect for you.

BEN: There's no need.

FRANÇOIS: They went to bed ages ago.

BEN: Sure, but I wouldn't want to …

FRANÇOIS: You'd get some peace.

*Pause.*

BEN: I suppose it would be quieter.

FRANÇOIS: You could even sleep in there if you want.

BEN: I could. *(Pause.)* Wouldn't they mind?

FRANÇOIS: They'll be delighted to have you there for breakfast.

BEN: Really?

FRANÇOIS: Maman will be thrilled.

ALICE: It's true, she'll love that.

FRANÇOIS: They'll actually be disappointed if you don't go.

BEN: Will they?

ALICE: It'd be a real shame.

FRANÇOIS: Mustn't let them down.

BEN: I don't want to let them down. *(Pause.)* Where would you sleep though?

FRANÇOIS: On here [the settee].

ALICE: It's not very comfortable.

BEN: *(To ALICE.)* It can't be too bad. You crash out on it every night virtually.

FRANÇOIS: It'll be perfect.

*Pause.*

ALICE: Or you could sleep in our bed if you'd rather.

FRANÇOIS: Maybe.

ALICE: Probably more comfortable. You wouldn't mind, Ben, would you?

BEN: Course not.

FRANÇOIS: Sure?

BEN: Absolutely.

ALICE: It really would be much more comfortable.

FRANÇOIS: Whatever you say. *(Silence.)* I'll give you the key.

*He takes out a key and gives it to BEN.*

BEN: Thanks.

FRANÇOIS: Have you been in our flat before?

BEN: No.

FRANÇOIS: It's exactly like yours, but the other way round.

BEN: Right.

FRANÇOIS: My room's the last on your left, at the end of the hall.

BEN: *(Indicating the hall in his flat.)* The hall …

FRANÇOIS: Yeah, but back to front.

BEN: Right, back to front.

FRANÇOIS: Just be a bit careful going in; the door creaks.

BEN: I'll watch it.

*Pause.*

ALICE: I hadn't thought of that.

BEN: What?

ALICE: Your flat's the other way round.

BEN: That's right.

ALICE: The same, but the other way round.

FRANÇOIS: Yes.

ALICE: I hadn't thought of that.

*Silence. All three look at each other.*

BEN: Right, well … goodnight.

FRANÇOIS: Night.

ALICE: See you tomorrow.

BEN: Yep.

*BEN goes out and shuts the door.*

*Blackout.*

## SCENE TWELVE

*Next morning, Ben stands in the doorway. FRANÇOIS is flicking through a newspaper in the lounge. Both men are in dressing gowns and each holds a mug of coffee.*

FRANÇOIS: What do you reckon to Maman's coffee?

BEN: Excellent. How about Alice's?

FRANÇOIS: It's a bit strong, but I'll get used to it.

BEN: Get used to anything. *(Pause. They each take a sip of coffee at the same time.)* I put your dressing gown on. Hope you don't mind.

FRANÇOIS: Not at all. I've put yours on.

BEN: Quite right. *(Pause.)* Comfy?

FRANÇOIS: Lovely fabric.

BEN: It's new. I just bought it.

FRANÇOIS: You can tell.

> *Silence. They sip simultaneously.*

BEN: Decent night's sleep?

FRANÇOIS: Excellent. Your bed's really comfortable.

BEN: Great. We were thinking of maybe getting something a bit bigger.

FRANÇOIS: No need.

BEN: Really?

FRANÇOIS: It's just right as it is.

> *Silence. Simultaneous sips. ALICE comes in. She's wearing her dressing gown.*

BEN: Morning.

ALICE: Sleep well?

BEN: Yeah. You?

ALICE: Very.

*ALICE gets herself some coffee.*

ALICE: More coffee?

FRANÇOIS: No thanks.

ALICE: Ben?

BEN: I prefer Juliette's.

*JULIETTE comes out of her flat and gives BEN a peck on the cheek. ALICE sits beside FRANÇOIS with her coffee.*

JULIETTE: Such a lovely surprise to wake up this morning and find little Ben in our midst.

BEN: My pleasure.

JULIETTE: I made him pancakes. Good weren't they?

BEN: They were fantastic.

JULIETTE: I do love making pancakes.

*ALICE, FRANÇOIS and BEN take a sip of coffee simultaneously.*

GILLES: *(Calling from the other flat.)* Juliette? Is there any more coffee?

JULIETTE: No, Ben drank it all.

BEN: *(Calls out.)* Sorry, Gilles!

GILLES: No problem. I'll do some more.

*Pause.*

BEN: Can I come in?

ALICE: Of course.

FRANÇOIS: Make yourself at home.

*BEN comes in. GILLES comes out of the other flat and joins JULIETTE in the doorway.*

JULIETTE: Wasn't it lovely to have Ben with us this morning?

GILLES: Lovely.

JULIETTE: We should do it more often.

FRANÇOIS: We should do it all the time.

GILLES: Good idea.

*BEN looks at JULIETTE and GILLES, obviously very happy.*

GILLES: May we come in?

FRANÇOIS: *(Snarls.)* No!

*Still looking at JULIETTE and GILLES, FRANÇOIS puts his arm around ALICE's shoulders. Short silence.*

GILLES: Fine, fine.

JULIETTE: Lovely.

*FRANÇOIS hugs ALICE tighter. JULIETTE and GILLES watch for a moment then go back into their flat. FRANÇOIS starts to kiss ALICE, gently at first but with increasing passion. BEN enjoys his coffee with visible satisfaction. After a moment, he observes FRANÇOIS and ALICE's clinch with no emotion whatever.*

BEN: I'll get those out of your way. Make things a bit easier.

*He takes the coffee cups from their hands. FRANÇOIS and ALICE stretch out on the settee still kissing. BEN stands watching impassively.*

BEN: Right … I'm off back to my room. Lot of work waiting for me. *(He carries on watching them. Their embraces are increasingly violent, almost animalistic.)* Don't get up, I'll see myself out.

*After a moment, he exits.*

*Blackout.*

## SCENE THIRTEEN

*ALICE and FRANÇOIS in the lounge.*

ALICE: You're the one who said …

FRANÇOIS: I said we should maybe do something, not throw a …

ALICE: Too late.

FRANÇOIS: Not throw a party.

ALICE: It's not a party.

FRANÇOIS: You should have asked me.

ALICE: I didn't even invite them, they invited themselves.

FRANÇOIS: Brilliant!

ALICE: What?

FRANÇOIS: We'll never get rid of them.

ALICE: *(Suddenly disconcerted.)* Hang on …

FRANÇOIS: We'll have to move out to shake them off.

ALICE: You've said that before.

FRANÇOIS: What?

ALICE: You've said that before.

FRANÇOIS: You know I don't like them.

ALICE: We've had this conversation before.

FRANÇOIS: I don't want them round here.

ALICE: The same conversation, I mean. The same words. Exactly the same.

FRANÇOIS: That's impossible. *(They stare at each other.)* You're imagining things.

*ALICE snatches a picture frame from the sideboard and hurls it violently at FRANÇOIS. He just avoids it and it smashes against the wall. Silence. BEN opens the door of the flat. He sees ALICE and FRANÇOIS then stops in embarrassment. They all look at each other.*

BEN: Sorry. So stupid … wrong door.

ALICE: Don't worry.

BEN: Must have been daydreaming.

FRANÇOIS: Yeah.

ALICE: The doors are the same. Easily done.

BEN: I suppose coming into your home is such an automatic thing you don't even notice if you've gone into someone else's.

*Pause.*

FRANÇOIS: Just … be careful it doesn't happen again.

BEN: Absolutely.

ALICE: It's all right, François.

FRANÇOIS: We just have to be careful.

BEN: You're absolutely right. I'm sorry. In future …

FRANÇOIS: *(Cutting him off.)* In future I'll bolt the door.

*Blackout.*

## SCENE FOURTEEN

*ALICE and FRANÇOIS side by side. BEN sits on the settee between JULIETTE and GILLES. Ben and the Gauches are dressed for travel. There are large, heavy looking suitcases by the door.*

ALICE: Again?

GILLES: Yes. A long trip …

ALICE: You do travel a lot.

JULIETTE: This time we have to go.

FRANÇOIS: What a pity.

ALICE: Will you be back soon?

GILLES: We don't have a set date for our return.

*Slight pause.*

FRANÇOIS: Are you going, Ben?

JULIETTE: Of course.

BEN: I love travel.

FRANÇOIS: That's good then.

*Slight pause.*

ALICE: I'm jealous. I'd like to travel.

JULIETTE: You want to leave here?

FRANÇOIS: No.

GILLES: Don't leave.

JULIETTE: You like it here.

FRANÇOIS: Enormously.

ALICE: It's nice here.

GILLES: Lovely flat.

BEN: It's exactly the kind of place I'd like.

*Pause.*

ALICE: Would you like a drink before you set off?

JULIETTE: I think we really should be going.

FRANÇOIS: Don't let us keep you.

*They all get up.*

GILLES: A pleasure.

*GILLES shakes FRANÇOIS's hand then goes to ALICE.*

ALICE: For us too.

*GILLES kisses ALICE's hand.*

GILLES: I'd love to have spent a bit more time with you. Another time maybe.

ALICE: Maybe.

JULIETTE: Take care of yourself, François.

FRANÇOIS: You too.

*After a moment's hesitation, JULIETTE embraces FRANÇOIS. He doesn't return it.*

GILLES: *(Heading to the door.)* Juliette.

JULIETTE: Coming.

*JULIETTE goes to the door. ALICE and BEN are face to face.*

ALICE: It's a shame. We never really got to know each other.

BEN: I'm sure we'll see each other again.

ALICE: Maybe.

*BEN kisses ALICE on both cheeks. As he starts to go, they look at each other oddly.*

BEN: What perfume's that?

ALICE: I'm not wearing any.

*Pause. They look at each other oddly.*

BEN: Weird. I thought I recognised …

JULIETTE: *(Cutting him off.)* Ben!

BEN: Yes?

JULIETTE: If we're not going to miss this flight

BEN: Coming.

ALICE: Let me get the door.

*She goes to the front door and opens it.*

GILLES: Goodbye.

ALICE: Have a good trip.

BEN: *(To ALICE.)* See you.

ALICE: See you.

*BEN hasn't moved. FRANÇOIS grabs BEN's bag up and breaks the deadlock, bundling Ben and all out of the door.*

FRANÇOIS: Let me give you a hand with these.

*All leave.*

*ALICE is on her own*

*Silence.*

*ALICE sits on the settee and closes her eyes.*

*The baby cries.*

ALICE: *(To herself.)* Not again

*ALICE starts for the hallway leading to the bedrooms. The crying gets louder and ALICE realises that it's not coming from the bedroom but from somewhere outside. She opens the front door and stands rigid in the doorway. The crying is coming from the flat opposite. She crosses the hall and puts her ear to their door. The crying gets louder. ALICE knocks gently at the door.*

ALICE: Is anyone there?

*She tries to open the door but it's locked.*

ALICE: Ben? Juliette? Gilles? It's Alice. Open up.

*She knocks more and more loudly.*

ALICE: Is there someone in there? Open up. Open this door! I think there's … Ben?

*The crying gets louder and ALICE starts to panic. She rattles at the door handle.*

ALICE: Oh please!… Somebody open the door! Open the door!

*She hammers at the door. We hear the loud, discordant sound of the child's toy as if someone were hitting the baby with it. ALICE freezes to hear what's going on. The noise of the toy gets more and more aggressive and the baby starts screaming. ALICE loses it completely. She tries to break the door down with her shoulder.*

ALICE: Oh please! Stop it! Stop it! Stop it!

*The noise stops dead.*
*ALICE very slowly backs away from the door into her own flat.*
*We hear footsteps approaching the door of the Gauche apartment.*
*The door handle of the Gauche apartment slowly turns.*
*ALICE rushes forward to her own door, slams it firmly shut and retreats once more downstage.*

*Her own door handle turns and shakes.*

*The door slowly opens to reveal FRANÇOIS who advances on ALICE who is downstage of the settee.*

*FRANÇOIS steps on the toy, which gives off its loud discordant noise. FRANÇOIS bends down gently and picks it up.*

ALICE: I forgot to put it away.

*FRANÇOIS doesn't move.*

*Silence.*

*ALICE looks toward the bedroom corridor then back to FRANÇOIS.*

ALICE: I'm going to lie down.

FRANÇOIS: Good plan. You look tired.

ALICE: Do I?

FRANÇOIS: You look a bit … absent … far away.

*They look at each other.*

FRANÇOIS: 'Night.

ALICE: You too.

*ALICE starts to go. FRANÇOIS gets a book from the pile still on the floor then sits on the settee.*

ALICE: What are you doing?

FRANÇOIS: Don't know. Might read for a bit.

*Pause.*

ALICE: I'm off to bed.

FRANÇOIS: I know.

ALICE: …

FRANÇOIS: I'm not stopping you.

*The baby starts crying. ALICE glances down the corridor.*

ALICE: I'd quite like to be on my own.

FRANÇOIS: You want me to sleep in here?

*Pause.*

ALICE: Can you go, please?

FRANÇOIS: Huh?

ALICE: I just want you to go.

FRANÇOIS: I don't really feel like going out.

ALICE: I want you to go home.

FRANÇOIS: Where?

ALICE: Home.

FRANÇOIS: Home?

ALICE: Yes, home, with your parents …

FRANÇOIS: My parents?

ALICE: Just go home.

FRANÇOIS: I am home.

*The crying gets louder still.*

ALICE: Look, François, I don't want to …

FRANÇOIS: Have a lie down Alice, go on.

ALICE: Get out please.

FRANÇOIS: What's wrong with you?

ALICE: Get out!

FRANÇOIS: And go where?

ALICE: Home.

FRANÇOIS: This is our home.

ALICE: Stop it.

FRANÇOIS: *(Getting up.)* This is where I live.

ALICE: No! This is where I live.

FRANÇOIS: With you.

ALICE: You live with your parents.

FRANÇOIS: *(Moving gently towards her.)* Hey, that's not fair. I lost my parents a long time ago. Just go and look in on your son …

ALICE: My son?

FRANÇOIS: Go and see the little man …

ALICE: What are you talking about?

FRANÇOIS: … who's been crying for five minutes now.

ALICE: My son is …

FRANÇOIS: He needs you, Alice.

ALICE: No, my son is …

FRANÇOIS: In his room.

ALICE: Stop!

FRANÇOIS: Probably just hungry.

ALICE: Don't you dare talk about my son.

FRANÇOIS: He wants his Maman.

ALICE: You've never seen him. You know nothing about him.

FRANÇOIS: We have a son, Alice.

ALICE: No.

> *The baby still crying.*

ALICE: Go away.

FRANÇOIS: Alice …

ALICE: Go away.

FRANÇOIS: It's me.

ALICE: I want you out of here!

FRANÇOIS: *(Trying to calm her.)* It's me, François. Your husband.

> *FRANÇOIS holds her in his arms. She doesn't respond.*
>
> *He gently lets go of ALICE and heads off down the corridor.*

ALICE: *(After him.)* You're the neighbour. You're just my neighbour.

FRANÇOIS: *(Heading off.)* We're married.

ALICE: You live opposite.

FRANÇOIS: *(Off.)* We have a six month old son …

ALICE: Across the hall.

FRANÇOIS: (*Returning from off.*) … who's crying his eyes out.

ALICE: In the flat across the hall.

> *FRANÇOIS reenters holding a six month old baby in his arms.*
> *ALICE slowly backs away, and sits on the settee.*
> *FRANÇOIS joins her on the settee, maybe some small talk with the baby.*
> *ALICE watches.*
> *FRANÇOIS looks at ALICE, and decides to hand the baby to her.*
>
> *ALICE takes the child, at first gingerly, and, very slowly, holds it close.*
>
> *Pause.*
>
> *She suddenly turns to look at FRANÇOIS: He holds her gaze.*
>
> *Both sit back and look at the child, and look at each other, and look ahead.*
>
> *SLOW FADE TO BLACK.*

*END.*

WWW.OBERONBOOKS.COM

Follow us on www.twitter.com/@oberonbooks
& www.facebook.com/OberonBooksLondon